Modern Critical Interpretations

William Shakespeare's Measure for Measure

Modern Critical Interpretations

These and other titles in preparation

Modern Critical Interpretations

William Shakespeare's
Measure for Measure

Edited and with an introduction by

Harold Bloom
Sterling Professor of the Humanities
Yale University

Chelsea House Publishers ◊ *1987*
NEW YORK ◊ NEW HAVEN ◊ PHILADELPHIA

© 1987 by Chelsea House Publishers,
a division of Chelsea House Educational Communications, Inc.,
95 Madison Avenue, New York, NY 10016
345 Whitney Avenue, New Haven, CT 06511
5014 West Chester Pike, Edgemont, PA 19028

Introduction © 1987 by Harold Bloom

Printed and bound in the United States of America

∞ The paper used in this publication meets the minimum
requirements of the American National Standard for Permanence
of Paper for Printed Library Materials, Z39.48-1984.

Library of Congress Cataloging-in-Publication Data
William Shakespeare's measure for measure.
  (Modern critical interpretations)
  Bibliography: p.
  Includes index.
  Summary: A collection of critical essays on
Shakespeare's problematical comedy "Measure for
Measure" arranged in chronological order of
publication.
  1. Shakespeare, William, 1564–1616. Measure for
measure. [1. Shakespeare, William, 1564–1616. Measure
for measure. 2. English literature—History and
criticism] I. Bloom, Harold. II. Series.
PR2824.W49 1987   822.3′3   87–8090
ISBN 0-87754-931-1 (alk. paper)

Contents

Editor's Note

This book gathers together a representative selection of the best modern criticism of Shakespeare's problematical comedy *Measure for Measure*. The critical essays are reprinted here in the chronological sequence of their original publication. I am grateful to Susanna Gilbert for her aid in editing this volume.

My introduction meditates upon the equivocal but powerful speeches on death delivered by the disguised Duke and by Claudio, against the background of Barnardine's refusal to die. M. C. Bradbrook begins the chronological sequence of criticism by arguing for the deliberateness of Shakespeare's strange insights into authority, truth, and justice in *Measure for Measure*. In a very different vein, Harold C. Goddard, the most imaginative of modern Shakespeareans, views the play as a radical subversion of power and authority in any era.

A. P. Rossiter, another quirky critic who continues to illuminate Shakespeare, asserts that *Measure for Measure* transcends Christianity and history and becomes a permanent inquisition into human nature. I agree with Rossiter that Walter Pater's essay on the play remains a valuable guide to aspects of *Measure for Measure* that more normative critics have neglected.

Arguing that we ought to read the play as a joyous and mocking comedy, Herbert Weil, Jr., contrasts interestingly with Harriett Hawkins, to whom *Measure for Measure* seems a dark demonstration "that God's temple itself may contain the Devil's chapel." Louise Schleiner, starting with an acknowledgment of the play's chameleon quality, reads *Measure for Measure* as "a comedy of a well-intentioned ruler with the rather quixotic notion of actually imitating the New Testament God in his government."

The art of not dying is invoked as the play's particular art by Phoebe S. Spinrad, after which Marcia Riefer concludes this volume with an analysis of Isabella as "Shakespeare's pivotal female figure," a prolepsis of the return of female power in the late romances, where "patriarchal and misogynistic values" are supposedly again subverted, as they may have been in the early comedies.

Introduction

I

Northrop Frye observes that among all the principal characters of *Measure for Measure,* only Lucio seems sane. I would add the spectacular Barnardine, who sensibly judges that in the mad world of this drama, the only way to avoid execution is to stay safely asleep. If you fall into the error of applying moral realism to *Measure for Measure,* then you will conclude that the Duke, Angelo, Claudio, Isabella, and Mariana all are crazy, with the Duke the craziest of all. Clearly, the play is a fantastic story, a deliberate wildness, as outrageous as *Twelfth Night* or *The Winter's Tale.*

Measure for Measure seems to cohere only as a kind of erotic romance, a very original kind. Though it achieves plausibility only within the parameters of its curious assumptions, those assumptions are not so much Elizabethan conventions as they are purely Shakespearean. If they seem not so curious to us, that is because we live on them still, because as mimetic conventions they have become our assumptions and help govern our expectations as to what it is that makes verbal representation convincing to us.

The Duke's manipulations, though ultimately (and rather mechanically) benign in their effects, are as theatrical and amoral as Iago's or Edmund's, and his motivations always must remain inscrutable. He interests us only in relation to his views on death, which is Claudio's only claim upon our interest also. Since Angelo, on close scrutiny, is what we might now call a case history, that leaves only Isabella, who indeed is interesting, all too interesting. Her militant chastity is the play's center, the origin of its mode of producing meaning.

To remark of Isabella that she is unsympathetic is obvious, all too obvious, but then the Duke, Angelo, Claudio, and even poor Mariana are in their ways unsympathetic also. That only the obsessive slanderer Lucio and the dissolute Barnardine attract us makes clear the deliberate estrangement of Shakespearean representation in this play. The gap between natural being and role-playing in the Duke and Angelo is absolute, while in Isabella it is almost frightening. Lucio and Barnardine win us because they are precisely what they present themselves as being.

When I think of *Measure for Measure* I first remember Barnardine and then Lucio among the characters, but the speeches that come first to mind are all from act 3, scene 1, in which the Duke, Claudio, and Isabella all manifest preternatural eloquence and simultaneously descend even lower in our esteem. I sometimes believe that the most sublime passage of all in Shakespeare is the Duke's astonishing speech in reply to Claudio's: "I have hope to live, and am prepar'd to die." Yet what could be more problematic than this surpassing rhetorical persuasiveness spoken in a supposed comedy by a ruling figure to someone absurdly condemned to death? And this is rendered yet more dubious by the speaker's duplicity, since he is peculiarly disguised as a friar and yet clearly does not offer anything like Christian comfort:

> DUKE: Be absolute for death: either death or life
> Shall thereby be the sweeter. Reason thus with life:
> If I do lose thee, I do lose a thing
> That none but fools would keep. A breath thou art,
> Servile to all the skyey influences,
> That dost this habitation where thou keep'st
> Hourly afflict. Merely, thou art death's fool,
> For him thou labor'st by thy flight to shun,
> And yet run'st toward him still. Thou art not noble,
> For all th' accommodations that thou bear'st
> Are nurs'd by baseness. Thou'rt by no means valiant,
> For thou dost fear the soft and tender fork
> Of a poor worm. Thy best of rest is sleep,
> And that thou oft provok'st, yet grossly fear'st
> Thy death, which is no more. Thou art not thyself,
> For thou exists on many a thousand grains
> That issue out of dust. Happy thou art not,
> For what thou hast not, still thou striv'st to get,
> And what thou hast, forget'st. Thou art not certain,
> For thy complexion shifts to strange effects,

After the moon. If thou art rich, thou'rt poor,
For like an ass, whose back with ingots bows,
Thou bear'st thy heavy riches but a journey,
And death unloads thee. Friends hast thou none,
For thine own bowels, which do call thee [sire],
The mere effusion of thy proper loins,
Do curse the gout, sapego, and the rheum
For ending thee no sooner. Thou hast nor youth nor age,
But as it were an after-dinner's sleep,
Dreaming on both, for all thy blessed youth
Becomes as aged, and doth beg the alms
Of palsied eld; and when thou art old and rich,
Thou hast neither heat, affection, limb, nor beauty,
To make thy riches pleasant. What's yet in this
That bears the name of life? Yet in this life
Lie hid moe thousand deaths; yet death we fear
That makes these odds all even.

(ll. 5–41)

Most of the great speeches in Shakespeare gain, as they should, by being read or delivered in context, but this is enormously more powerful and dignified when we rip it away from the play and forget both situation and speaker. What does that tell us about the dialectical interplay of Shakespearean representation and Shakespearean rhetoric? Here the strength of representation is at best equivocal in its force, since we cannot accept the reality of this speech as comfort, intended or actual, and even wonder if Claudio is not being ironical when he begins his reply with "I humbly thank you." Northrop Frye dryly remarks that the speech urges Claudio to "welcome death because if he lives he may get a lot of uncomfortable diseases." As addressed to a young man that is silly, but out of context I suggest the speech naturally falls into the mode in which each of us addresses him- or herself. As a meditation of the self directed to the self, the lines become at once bracing and elegiac, until they achieve an extraordinary triumph in a passage that haunted T. S. Eliot, who made them the epigraph to his "Gerontion," and that deeply engaged Dr. Samuel Johnson:

Thou has nor youth nor age,
But as it were an after-dinner's sleep,
Dreaming on both.

Johnson memorably commented:

> This is exquisitely imagined. When we are young we busy
> ourselves in forming schemes for succeeding time, and miss
> the gratifications that are before us; when we are old we
> amuse the languour of age with the recollection of youthful
> pleasures or performances; so that our life, of which no part
> is filled with the business of the present time, resembles our
> dreams after dinner, when the events of the morning are
> mingled with the designs of the evening.

"Dinner," to Shakespeare and to Johnson, was the midday meal
we now call lunch. Johnson, with his keen sense that human life was
everywhere a condition in which much was to be endured and little to
be enjoyed, reads in Shakespeare's lines the profound representation of
our perpetual inability to live in the present moment. Caught as we are
between wistfulness and nostalgia, never-to-come future and illusory
past, the afternoon and morning of our existence, we confound midday with evening. Johnson has uncovered one of *Measure for Measure's*
uncanniest ranges of meaning: its protagonists' joys are either completed or deferred, and only the disreputable Lucio and Barnardine are
alive in the present. If the immediacy of the moment is available only
to the dissolute, then we see the malady that has crazed the Duke's
Vienna, a mad city indeed.

Lucio, though sane, has nothing about him that is not rank, while
the outrageous Barnardine is not only the sane foil to nearly the entire
personae but is admirably vital, somewhat in the mode of that greatest
of vitalists, Sir John Falstaff, though Barnardine is no wit. His fundamental recourse is sleep: "He will not wake," and when they insist
upon waking him, he sublimely remarks: "I swear I will not die to-day
for any man's persuasion." We like the Duke best, at the end, when he
pardons Barnardine, thus giving the triumph to the most humane
sentiment in the play, Barnardine's: "I will not consent to die this day,
that's certain."

What is least humane in *Measure for Measure* is not even Angelo,
let alone the enigmatic Duke, but Isabella. I cannot agree with Anne
Barton's observation that "like Angelo, she has arrived at a new and
juster knowledge of herself" by the drama's end. She seems not so
much changed as distracted, while Angelo's new and just knowledge is
just that he has been found out! Shakespeare in *Measure for Measure*
cares not a jot for our moral outrage, or else he delights in provoking

it. Consider the shock of juxtaposition he gives us between Claudio's eloquent fear and Isabella's sadistic display of enraged virtue:

CLAUDIO: Death is a fearful thing.
ISABELLA: And shamed life a hateful.
CLAUDIO: Ay, but to die, and go we know not where;
 To lie in cold obstruction, and to rot;
 This sensible warm motion to become
 A kneaded clod; and the delighted spirit
 To bathe in fiery floods, or to reside
 In thrilling region of thick-ribbed ice;
 To be imprison'd in the viewless winds
 And blown with restless violence round about
 The pendant world; or to be worse than worst
 Of those that lawless and incertain thought
 Imagine howling—'tis too horrible!
 The weariest and most loathed worldly life
 That age, ache, [penury], and imprisonment
 Can lay on nature is a paradise
 To what we fear of death.
ISABELLA: Alas, alas!
CLAUDIO: Sweet sister, let me live.
 What sin you do to save a brother's life,
 Nature dispenses with the deed so far,
 That it becomes a virtue.
ISABELLA: O you beast!
 O faithless coward! O dishonest wretch!
 Wilt thou be made a man out of my vice?
 Is't not a kind of incest, to take life
 From thine own sister's shame? What should I think?
 Heaven shield my mother play'd my father fair!
 For such a warped slip of wilderness
 Ne'er issu'd from his blood. Take my defiance!
 Die, perish! Might but my bending down
 Reprieve thee from thy fate, it should proceed.
 I'll pray a thousand prayers for thy death,
 No word to save thee.
CLAUDIO: Nay, hear me, Isabel.

            (ll. 115–147)

Whether or not there is a Dantesque overtone in Claudio's extraordinary speech on the fear of death, we now hear Milton in it, since it prefigures much that is Satanic in *Paradise Lost*, and something that is Belial's there as well. Johnson, whose imagination was so stirred by the prospect of death, did not comment on this speech, perhaps because it moved him too strongly. Of Isabella's harsh reaction, Johnson noted that we ought to "consider her not only as a virgin but a nun," to which one must rejoin that nuns do not marry dukes. Frye points to an obsession with the figure of the father in Isabella's rhetoric, which is certainly there, but the horror of incest is even more direct:

> Wilt thou be made a man out of my vice?
> Is't not a kind of incest, to take life
> From thine own sister's shame?

Evidently Isabella can envision coitus only as incest, but that is the dark, central insight of the play, if it can be called insight. Vienna in *Measure for Measure* is Isabella's vision; she defines its mode and its ambiance. Her passional life is a deferred torment, and the entire drama can be regarded as her version of the return of the repressed. She does not speak at all during the last eighty-five lines of the long scene in the act that ends the play and we do not even know that she definitely will accept the Duke's offer of marriage. Nor do we know how to interpret the final speech she makes, when she joins Mariana in pleading for Angelo's life: "Thoughts are no subjects, / Intents but merely thoughts." If a murderous intention, like Angelo's, is not answerable to justice, then presumably incestuous desires also need not be subject to a moral or spiritual authority. When I think of *Measure for Measure,* my final thought is always of Isabella, who is neither likeable nor endless to meditation, but who is finally more problematical even than the Duke, in this most problematic of all of Shakespeare's plays.

Authority, Truth, and Justice in *Measure for Measure*

M. C. Bradbrook

> *Judge not, that ye be not judged.*
> *For with what judgment ye judge, ye shall be judged: and with what measure*
> *ye mete it shall be measured to you again.*
>
> (MATT. 8:1–2)

This play is more theoretical than most of Shakespeare's writings, less easy, without his accustomed refusal to theorise or analyse. It differs from *Troilus and Cressida*, the problems of which are epistemological, and the method therefore impersonal but elaborate. In *Measure for Measure* the problems are ethical, and concern conduct rather than belief: the style is barer, sharper, and harder, the language simpler and plainer, and the characters allegorical rather than symbolical. The method, however, is akin to that of *Troilus and Cressida* in being largely based upon the debate: not the massed public debate, but the naked antagonism of conflict, as between Isabel and Angelo, Claudio and Isabel, and Claudio and the Duke.

In this play Shakespeare adopts a technique as analytic as that of Donne to something resembling the late medieval Morality. It might be named The Contention between Justice and Mercy, or False Authority unmasked by Truth and Humility; Angelo stands for Authority and for Law, usurping the place of the Duke, who is not only the representative of Heavenly Justice but of Humility, whilst Isabel represents both Truth and Mercy.

The first necessity is to grasp the importance of the Duke. Histori-

From *The Review of English Studies* 17, no. 68 (October 1941) © 1941 by Oxford University Press.

cally he belongs to a familiar dramatic type; that of the omnipotent disguised character who directs the intrigue, often hearing strange things of himself by the way—the type of Malevole, Vindice, the husband in *Eastward Ho!* and the father in *Englishmen for My Money*, a type to which the early Hamlet perhaps also belonged. Wilson Knight sees in him a Christlike figure come from a far country to save Vienna: all powerful, all merciful, and perhaps in his marriage to Isabel only ratifying her position as the Bride of the Church. It is certain that the Duke is more than the average disguised puppet master of which Brainworm is the best known example: he is at least the representative of Heavenly Justice.

> I percieue, your grace, like powre diuine
> Hath look'd vpon my passes.

says Angelo. But as the play was written for performance at Court in 1604, it is possible that he also represents that pillar of justice, the British Solomon, James I, still in the first flush of popularity. Several compliments to his humility and dislike of crowds are palpably meant for the ear of James (1.1.67–72; 2.4.28–31).

No idea was more stressed by Elizabethan playwrights than that Justice lay in the hands of the magistrate, as God's vicegerent on earth. Hence Lord Chancellor Bacon deprecated Revenge, "a kind of wild Justice," even in cases where the magistrate cannot or will not act.

As the Duke represents unerring Justice, and in his readiness to live as a poor Friar, helping his meanest and most criminal subjects, represents also Humility as it resides in true authority; so Isabel stands for unerring Truth, and Truth is always merciful.

> How would you be,
> If he which is the top of Iudgement should
> But iudge you, as you are?
>
> (2.2.75–77)

she asks Angelo. The marriage of Truth and Justice resolves the frenzy of lies, prevarications, truths and half-truths which in the last scene records the hollowness of all external judgment, even as in *The Faerie Queene*, the marriage of Truth and Holiness, in the persons of Una and the Red Cross Knight, defeats the calumnious and evil forces represented by Duessa and Archimago.

Angelo stands for the letter of the Law, for a false Authority: he also stands for Seeming or False Semblant. At the very moment he is about to tempt Isabel he says:

> I (now the voyce of the recorded Law)
> Pronounce a sentence on your Brothers life.
>
> (2.4.62–63)

But Authority is arbitrary (why pick out Claudio?), it apes a state unfit for humanity, encourages hidden vice in its own representative by endowing him with arbitrary power, and strives to overthrow truth and justice.

Claudio and Juliet stand for human nature, original sin; Mariana for *eros* (as distinct from *agape*); Barnardine is contrasted with Claudio to show how much below panic-struck egoism is mere brute insensibility. Juliet, whom Claudio "wrong'd," is penitent from the first and therefore absolved by the Duke; nor apparently does she ever stand in peril of her life, and she is not given a judgment in the final scene as all the others are. In the last scene measure for measure is meted out to all; not, perhaps, their measure according to earthly law—for Barnardine is pardoned—but the measure best devised to save their souls. The main purpose of the scene is to bring Angelo to repentance, and to achieve it against so strong a character terrific pressure has to be brought to bear. The Duke, who is as ruthlessly efficient in his means as he is benevolent in his ends, proceeds to apply the third degree with the skill of a grand inquisitor: and to this end he is ready to inflict any temporary suffering on Mariana and Isabel. Had they known his purpose they would have accepted the situation readily—Isabel from charity and Mariana from affection. Before the scene opens, Isabel complains that she must dissemble—"I would say the truth" (4.4.2)—but the Friar has told her it is "bitter to sweet end." The technique is only an advance upon the enacted lie of Mariana's visit, and that the Duke has justified beforehand: "Craft against vice I must applie" (3.2.299). He is naturally a merciful character; in theory he can condemn Barnardine, but when he actually sees the murderer, "A creature unpre-par'd, vnmeet for death," he realizes "To transport him in the minde he is, Were damnable" (4.3.75–76). It is not Shakespeare's relenting before the miracle of his own creation, as the critics have somtimes stated, which reprieves Barnardine—in this play Shakespeare is hardly in a relenting mood—but the Duke's instinctive revolt from applying the penalties of the law without regard to their consequences. He gives Barnardine to

Friar Peter to receive religious instruction, for he anticipates the maxim of Kant, and considers every human being as an end and never as a means, whether a means to the demonstration of the law or to other ends.

The debate between Justice and Mercy, which is the main theme of the play—see especially 2.2. and 5.1.—is conducted mainly between Isabel and Angelo, for of the Duke it might be said as it was of archetype and ectype in *The Faerie Queene:*

> "He merciful is, but Mercy's self is she"
> (FQ 2.9.43)

This debate can also be seen as a debate between Law and Religion, of which Angelo and Isabel are by profession the representatives. The Duke as secular head of the state is bound to punish not only offences but the offenders: yet Christianity, which he also professes, bids condemnation of the sin, not the sinner. "Judge not that ye be not judged. . . ." "Forgive us our trespasses. . . ." "Unto seventy times seven. . . ." The two sides of his dilemma are stated by Isabel and Angelo:

> I haue a brother is condemn'd to die,
> I doe beseech you let it be his fault,
> And not my brother
>
> . . . .
>
> Condemne the fault, and not the actor of it,
> Why, euery fault's condemned ere it be done:
> Mine were the verie Cipher of a Function
> (2.2.34–39)

On the other hand, Angelo's "devilish mercy" is, as the Duke sees, the very converse of true forgiveness:

> When Vice makes Mercie; Mercie's so extended,
> That for the faults loue, is th' offender friended.
> (4.2.115–6)

Yet Isabel pardons Angelo when he is forfeit to the law, and asks the Duke to pardon him also. The Duke deliberately reminds her of the *lex talionis,* as well as appealing to all her feelings of rage and resentment: "He dies for *Claudio's* death" (5.1.444). Yet although Isabel's first and natural impulse on hearing of her brother's execution had been "Oh, I wil to him, and plucke out his eies!" she kneels "in mercy of this fact," and perhaps it is this, rather than any of the Duke's ingenious tortures, which finally breaks the spirit of Angelo, though—an exquisite touch—only to the applying of his own legal standard to himself.

> And so deepe . . . sticks it in my penitent heart,
> That I craue death more willingly then mercy,
> 'Tis my deseruing, and I doe entreat it.
>
> (5.1.476–78)

The retributive aspect of criminal law seems always to have distressed Shakespeare. The cry of the tragedies is "None does offend, I say: none," and in the final plays the penalties of the law are waived for the most flagrant evildoers—Iachimo, Alonzo, Sebastian. The problem that a law to be just in general, must always be only an approximation to justice in particular cases, is stressed both by Claudio who suffers under it and the Duke who administers it.

> On whom it will, it will,
> On whom it will not (soe) yet still tis iust.
>
> (1.2.131–32)

> Lawes, for all faults,
> But faults so countenanc'd, that the strong Statutes
> Stand like the forfeites in a Barbers shop,
> As much in mocke, as marke.
>
> (5.1.317–20)

Yet here as in other plays Law in the sense of civil law is a constant subject of praise. Ulysses's speech in defence of order and degree (*Troilus and Cressida* 1.3.) is the most comprehensive eulogy, with its assimilation of human institutions, contracts and laws to the universal order of times and seasons. In *Henry IV, Part 2,* the Lord Chief Justice stands as the embodiment of everything that's excellent, and clearly represents civil law. He is the real antagonist of Falstaff, and it is he whom King Henry V admits as "a father to my youth" (5.2.118) after the judge has made his noble defence of his own act in committing to prison "the immediate heir of England."

> I then did vse the Person of your Father
>
> .   .   .   .
>
> Your Highnesse pleased to forget my place,

> The Maiesty, and power of Law, and Iustice,
> The Image of the King, whom I presented,
> And strooke me in my very Seate of Iudgement.
>
> (5.2.73ff.)

This adoption seals the doom of Falstaff, the grey haired iniquity who was even then saying, "The Lawes of England are at my command'ment. Happie are they, which haue been my Friendes: and woe vnto my Lord Chiefe Iustice!" (5.3.140–43).

No doubt for the purposes of the stage the Lord Chief Justice walked around in Eastcheap in full robes of office, and he is in a sense the pivot of the play, Henry IV being shown as a weak and dying man, a father rather than a king.

In *Measure for Measure* civil law enters the story chiefly through the marriage contracts. Juliet and Mariana are both contracted: Claudio says,

> Vpon a true contract
> I got possession of *Iulietas* bed,
> You know the Lady, she is fast my wife,
> Saue that we doe the denunciation lacke
> Of outward Order
>
> (1.2.155–59)

which was deferred for financial reasons. It is not clear whether this was a marriage "per verba de praesenti," as was the Duchess of Malfi's; if so, the child would be legitimate, as the union was customary, and neither party could have married elsewhere according to the English law and habit. Nevertheless the marriage was not regular, and in Chapman's continuation of *Hero and Leander* it may be seen what immense stress was laid on the public nature of the marriage contract, both in the vision of the goddess Ceremony, who descends to rebuke Hero, and in the Tale of Teras, which is a glorification of the social aspect of marriage.

Mariana was publicly affianced "as strongly as words could make up vows" (5.1.220–21), and the marriage settlements had been actually drawn up. Angelo is therefore her "combynate husband," and the Duke envisages that the result of their union may be a child whose existence will "compell him to her recompense" (3.1.263–64). The fact that the contract had been public and approved by the lady's friends would weigh very strongly with the Elizabethans, for to steal a marriage was almost a misdemeanour, as the case of the Duchess of Malfi demonstrated.

Isabella is the Bride of the Church, and to the horror of proposed violation Angelo adds a direct crime against religion. As a novice she is as it were betrothed, and apparently on the eve of her "approbation." If she were a novice she would be subject to the authority of the Mother, would wear the novice's dress, and obey the Rule, which was that of the Poor Clares, an order of great poverty, seclusion, and austerity, reformed into still further strictness by the work of St. Colette (ca. 1400) and the Capuchines (ca. 1540). Isabel's vows should have been taken between her first and second interview with Angelo; in the second, she is introduced as "One *Isabell*, a Sister," and the Friar addresses her as "sister," in 3.1, a term he would not use to a novice; but if in the interval she had been given the first veil—it is scarcely likely that she was at a more advanced stage—she would hardly accuse herself publicly of incontinence, considering the disgrace to her order. It seems more reasonable that she should defer her vows, and that in the last scene she should appear in secular clothes, perhaps in mourning for Claudio. The Duke also appears again in secular habit, and changes of clothes had a strong effect upon the Elizabethan stage. An Isabel in a secular habit could be arrested with more propriety than an Isabel in a veil; and the final tableau also would look less unnatural.

Some indication of the Elizabethan view of marriage as a public contract rather than a private relationship may be gained, as has been said, from Chapman; though English youth was more free than that of most countries, the rule was still that marriage should be determined by social equality, family duty, and public advantage rather than by personal inclination. Juliet and Mariana are parallel in misfortune: in the view of the Friar Juliet is more guilty than Claudio, but in the view of Isabel the sin is Claudio's:

> Women? Helpe heauen: men their creation marre
> In profiting by them: Nay, call us ten times fraile,
> For we are soft, as our complexions are,
> And credulous to false prints.
>
> (2.4.128–31)

It is the old story, "Men have marble, women waxen minds," and their fatal vulnerability lies in their sympathetic natures: they lack judgment and intellectual detachment. Hence even the Duke adjures Claudio to marry her he has "wrong'd," and he insists on a full marriage ceremony for Mariana to "safe-guard" her "honor" against "Imputation" (5.1.420–23). Even Lucio, though forgiven for his other forfeits, is obliged to make an honest woman of Mistress Kate Keepdown. The four marriages represent, in descending order of dignity, variations upon this basic social contract. In *The Merchant of Venice*, a forerunner of this play in so many ways, the marriage contract is symbolized in the story of the rings, and contrasted with Shylock's purely legal bond. Marriage is the highest form of contract, in that it contains subtler possibilities for good, for evil, for variety than other types of contract: it not only imposes a legal obligation, but contains a promise of personal and general prosperity of the highest kind.

The basis of Justice and of Law is the establishment of truth. Perfect truth resides only in God: the devil is the father of lies, and in the current morality representations of him, his power of disguise, particularly of disguising himself as a virtue, was his subtlest weapon for the destruction of man. Hence the question of Truth apparent and real, of Falsehood conscious and unconscious is crucial to the plot. Shakespeare had before him the great visionary panorama of the first book of *The Faerie Queene*. This problem he had himself approached in *King Henry IV, Part 2*, where the prologue is spoken by Rumour "painted full of tongues." Rumour sets the tone for the play by appearing in this fashion: her nearest modern equivalent would be the Fairy Wish-Fulfillment. But the question of "Where lies Truth?" is not overtly debated. The contrast between True and False Seeming is stronger and more painful in *Troilus and Cressida*, where the whole tragedy of "True Troilus" turns on the gap between fact and imagination, Diomede's Cressida and his own: "If there be rule in unitie itselfe, This is not she." In *Measure for Measure*, the issue is prominent, but it is not a subject for debate or doubt. The main contrast between seeming and reality lies of course in "the prenzie Angelo," "the well-seeming Angelo," "this outward-sainted deputy." The Duke's first speech is an ironic comment on this:

> There is a kinde of Character in thy life
> That to th' obsseruer, doth thy history
> Fully vnfold.
>
> (1.1.27–28)

But it is made plain in the next scene . . . that the Duke is by no means reading Angelo's life in the accepted version.

The "seeming" of the deputy is echoed so often and so bitterly that to dwell on it would be tedious. Angelo has in him something of the dissembling power of Claudius King of Denmark, and also of his gnawing conscience; he is "At warre, twixt will and will not." Isabel, who, like Hamlet, "knows not 'seems' " but is forced to learn it, maintains the truth although Angelo's false outweighs her true: "Truth is truth To th' end of reckning" (5.1.44–45). After describing Angelo's "seeming," she concludes to the Duke:

> Let your reason serue
> To make the truth appeare, where it seemes hid,
> And hide the false seemes true.
>
> (5.1.65–67)

She is traduced as sorely as the Duke had been traduced by Lucio: yet she remains steadfast, more steadfast than the Duke would have been, for to him, as to Prospero, life itself is a dream and all its events but "seeming."

> Thou hast nor youth, nor age
> But as it were an after-dinners sleepe
> Dreaming on both.
>
> (3.1.32–34)

Yet the Duke is capable of turning every occasion to his own purpose, as in his ironic speech to Angelo on his return, which is designed to give a smart lash to the conscience of the deputy, and to express his own scepticism on "the vanity of wretched fooles."

> Giue me your hand,
> And let the Subiect see, to make them know
> That outward curtesies would faine proclaime
> Fauours that keepe within.
>
> (5.1.13–16)

On two occasions the Duke is surprised: he did not expect that Angelo would have Claudio executed, and he did not expect Isabel, to whom he had promised "revenges to your heart" (4.3.144), to forgive Angelo, though with his usual keenness he immediately seizes the opportunity to test the depth of her impulse.

Angelo himself upheld the doctrine of seeming. He admits to Escalus that a jury may contain worse criminals than the prisoner it condemns, yet the known crime must be punished.

> What knowes the Lawes
> That theeues do passe on theeues?
>
> (2.1.22–23)

But, he continues,

> When I, that censure him, do so offend,
> Let mine owne Iudgement patterne out my death.
>
> (2.1.29–30)

In this alone Angelo is not a seemer; he has the consistency to sentence himself.

> Immediate sentence then, and sequent death,
> Is all the grace I beg.
>
> (5.1.374–75)

In his fate, the Elizabethans would recognize the best and indeed the only true justice, that which is invoked by the title: Heaven's justice or Providence. They believed that justice could be left to the magistrate because if he were unable or unwilling to execute it, Heaven would deal justice to the evildoer. Whoever else forgot his contract God would not, and "Vengeance is mine, I will repay, saith the Lord."

The Duke, in his own way, is as great a seemer as Angelo. In his role as a poor Friar he is continually placed in ironic situations, his real and his seeming character being perpetually brought into conflict by unconscious words of Isabella, Escalus, the Provost, and Lucio—such phrases as "But (oh) how much is the good Duke deceiu'd in *Angelo*: if euer he returne, and I can speake to him, I will open my lips in vaine, or discouer his gouernment" (3.1.195–98). Some of the situations the Duke enjoys and more he turns to good account, but on one occasion he is rudely disillusioned. He had at least believed that the people loved him, and had retired only to preserve his reputation with them; yet he learns with cruel elaboration from Lucio how little a public man can claim immunity from slander. He is almost driven, in forgetfulness of his habit and his office alike, to challenge Lucio:

> DUKE: I am bound to call vppon you, and I pray you your
>   name?
> LUCIO: Sir my name is *Lucio*, wel known to the Duke.
>
> (3.2.171–73)

In the last scene he suffers defamation from the same quarter in his person as a Friar, when Lucio coolly puts into his own mouth all the slanders which he had been obliged to listen to. The Duke is wounded in his one vulnerable point, the dignity of his office, and it requires a second thought before he can pardon Lucio.

The difference between the Duke's seeming and that of Angelo is of course that the Duke's is purely an external change. In one sense he is a benevolent Haroun-al-Raschid; but his purposes are better than mere curiosity, and he is not defaming the cloak of religion.

> Come hither *Isabell*.
> Your *Frier* is now your Prince: As I was then,
> Aduertysing, and holy to your businesse,
> (Not changing heart with habit) I am still,
> Atturnied at your seruice.
>
> (5.1.382–86)

He who was greatest has been as a servant amongst them.

In the actions of Angelo, Isabel, and the Duke, the question of Truth and Seeming is stated, and they have thus a double burden of symbolism to carry. Nevertheless, the allegorical nature of *Measure for Measure* does not preclude a human interest in the characters. Though based perhaps on the Moralities, it is not a Morality. Angelo has always been recognized as a superb character study; Isabel and the Duke, though less impressive, are subtly presented. She is possibly the most intelligent of all Shakespeare's women; even poor Claudio recognizes her power in "reason and discourse" (1.2.196); yet she is young, and pitifully inexperienced. Outraged by Angelo's proposal, she turns to Claudio, the only man to whom she can turn—to ask for comfort as much as to give it:

> Ile to my brother,
> Though he hath falne by prompture of the blood,
> Yet hath he in him such a minde of Honor.
>
> (2.4.178–80)

But Claudio gives her an even crueller shock than Angelo had done, though to the eye of the spectator he is not without a case. He had had to listen to poor Isabel's bungled attempts at religious consolation. "Dar'st thou die?" she says, galling the sorest point with intolerable accuracy; and whereas the Friar had persuaded Claudio to at least temporary resignation, Isabella's efforts to "fit his mind to death" make him snarl very excusably:

> Why giue you me this shame?
> Think you I can a resolution fetch
> From flowrie tendernesse?
>
> (3.1.79–81)

Yet it is the same girl who cries to Claudio, "Die, perish!" and who cries, when he is in all appearance dead, for revenge on Angelo: "Oh, I wil to him, and plucke out his eies!" It is the same girl to whom Mariana appeals for help—

> They say best men are moulded out of faults—

and at that word Isabel, who not five minutes before had called Angelo a devil, recalls Claudio, recalls her own position as a suppliant for a dear but guilty life, and astounds even that skilled psychologist the Duke. Impulsively she kneels: intelligently she at once proceeds to justify the action. The garden house affair was after all an attempt to bribe Angelo, and he did not break the law in disregarding that illegal contract: "My Brother had but Iustice, In that he did the thing for which he dide." Whilst to the Duke, who had himself prevented Angelo's worst crime, she points out that Angelo is innocent before the law with respect to herself. It is a legal quibble worthy of Portia, and devised with the same speed as the sudden attempt to turn Angelo's attack upon herself to advantage:

> Signe me a present pardon for my brother,
> Or with an out-stretcht throate Ile tell the world aloud
> What man thou art.
>
> (2.4.153–55)

But while there the answer had been "Who will beleeue thee *Isabell*" (2.4.155), here justice recognizes, as Isabel points it out, the one grain of good in Angelo: "A due sinceritie governed his deedes, Till he did looke on me" (5.1.447–48). Having been overruled with regard to Angelo, the Duke proceeds to pardon Barnadine, Claudio, Lucio—though somewhat more reluctantly—and everybody else.

The Duke himself is a type of character whom Shakespeare did not often depict. His relations with his people are comparable with those of Henry V with Bates and Williams—Williams in particular is left rather in the position of Lucio; and, like Henry V, he can be extremely peremptory, is a born administrator, and enjoys probing and investigating into the lives of the common people—he would have appreciated Prince Hal's conversation with the drawer. On the other hand he more resembles Prospero in that all his actions are controlled by one purpose, in that complete self-confidence justifies his seeming cruelties (compare Prospero to Ferdinand), and in his almost unerring moral insight—being only twice deceived or surprised by other people's reactions. He resembles Prospero also in the absolute power which he maintains over the lives of the rest of the characters, except indeed the minor comic characters. These, the human sediment of Vienna, are not capable of being systematized: they exist independently of the moral framework and help further to give the play its naturalism and solidity. The difference between Pompey and Barnadine is the difference between a character and a portent—between the Artful Dodger and Bill Sikes.

In respect of the style, as of the plot, the structural pattern of main themes does not inhibit local energy, especially in the first part of the play. There are several images that run through the play, e.g., the "hidden ulcer,"—the dominant image of *Hamlet:* this is as it were the physical equivalent of the False Semblant, which skins and films the ulcerous places. There are also the images of great heat and cold: Angelo's blood is "Snow-broth"; Claudio fears the intense cold, the "thrilling Region of thicke-ribbed Ice" which may receive his soul after death; but on the whole there is comparatively little imagery after the third act. The acting possibilities of the latter half of the play are great; but it depends upon repetition and cross references. The nature of the writing here is fairly represented by Isabel's plea to the Duke. Angelo, accusing her of madness, says "she will speake most bitterly, and strange":

> ISABEL: Most strange: but yet most truly wil I speake,
> That *Angelo's* forsworne, is it not strange?
> That *Angelo's* a murtherer, is't not strange?
> That *Angelo* is an adulterous thiefe,
> An hypocrite, a virgin violator,
> Is it not strange? and strange?
> DUKE: Nay it is ten times strange?
> ISABEL: It is not truer he is *Angelo,*
> Then this is all as true, as it is strange;
> Nay, it is ten times true, for truth is truth
> To th' end of reckning.
>
> (5.1.37–46)

As conventional rhetoric depending on anaphora and epiphora, this is reminiscent of Constance or the Lady Anne rather than of the language of Shakespeare's maturity. However, it fits the dramatic situation—Isabel is almost in the position of a prosecuting counsel—and her own natural anger—she plays with the Duke's phrase as bitterly as she does with Angelo's. Beyond this, the full values of "true" and "strange," as they chime through the speech like the rhymes of a canzone, depend upon this being the finale of a great movement; the phrases take their value from their previous use, and the broad treatment here given to them is possible only because their full implications have been already worked out. This is more definitely illustrated in the Duke's consolation to Isabel for Claudio's supposed death.

> That life is better life past fearing death,
> Then that which liues to feare: make it your comfort,
> So happy is your Brother
>
> (5.1.398–400)

he says, condensing his great speech in 3.1. to an epigram.

The flattening out of the language in the latter half of this play is similar to the flattening out in *The Jew of Malta*, where Marlowe also began in a style rich and flexuous with imagery, and ended with a bare, "figurative," and comparatively prosaic speech. *Measure for Measure* remains a problem play, not because it is shallower, more unfinished or more incoherent than Shakespeare's other plays, but because it is stiffened by its doctrinaire and impersonal consideration of ethical values. The dryness, the pain behind the play, seem to depict a world in which external personal relationships are so hopelessly false and unreliable that it is necessary to cut below them to the moral substratum. To look for happiness is childish: what should be looked for is the good, proper, socially fitting relation; the basis is impersonal morality.

The relationships between justice and mercy, contract and fulfillment, appearance and reality are summed up in the relationship between earthly and heavenly justice; between the Duke in his secular and religious roles; between Isabel as a sister to her "vnhappie brother *Claudio*," and the bosom friend of Julietta, and Isabel as the sister to St. Clare among the "fasting Maides, whose mindes are dedicate to nothing temporall." When the Duke asks her hand he invokes her human sisterhood:

> "Giue me your hand, and say you will be mine,
> He is my brother too."
>
> (5.1.493–94)

It was a large charity in the Duke to accept Claudio, who is not exactly an eligible relative for the head of the state, and with whose failings he is particularly well acquainted. If this conclusion seems a trifle laboured in the working out, the play perhaps justifies it as the representation of a bitterness which could as yet find but little heart to conceive that triumph of the good which is most firmly asserted, and believed, but which was not to be fully embodied till eight years later in *The Tempest*. As a final check upon Shakespeare's intentions, it is of interest to see how he modified his source, Whetstone's *Promos and Cassandra* (1578). He invented almost the entire role of the Duke—it is for this reason that the understanding of the Duke's character becomes especially necessary—for in Whetstone's play the king appears only in the final scene to deliver judgment. He split the heroine Cassandra into two characters, Isabel and Mariana; for in the original Cassandra yields, comes to love Promos, in spite of his having seemingly presented her with the bleeding head of her brother, and finally pleads for his life because she loves him, and he is her husband. Shakespeare has made Isabel a nun, which adds a completely different complexion to Angelo's temptation: in Whetstone there are not only no religious characters, there is no invoking of any religious standards. Shakespeare has changed the story of Claudio, who as Andrugio was allowed to escape by the provost, the provost being alone responsible for the substituted head; in the final scene Andrugio delivers himself up to save Promos, in pity for his sister's misery. Finally, Shakespeare has added all the minor comic characters, and moralized the main story: adding, that is to say, the whole structure of themes. A careful comparison of Shakespeare's and Whetstone's plays is not required. Whetstone's is wretched drivel; but the baldest summary records how completely Shakespeare transformed a shallow and barbarous story. The purposive nature of these changes makes it seem very unlikely that *Measure for Measure* contains many accidental, idle or automatic incidents. If it is strange, it is because Shakespeare conceived it in that way. It is deliberately, if not dogmatically, set down. Perhaps its best commentator would have been Ben Jonson: it is one of the few of Shakespeare's writings of which he might wholeheartedly have approved.

Power in *Measure for Measure*

Harold C. Goddard

"Would you know a man? Give him power." History sometimes seems little else than an extended comment on that ancient maxim. Our own day has elucidated it on a colossal scale. *Measure for Measure* might have been expressly written to drive home its truth. It is little wonder, then, that the play of Shakespeare's in which the word "authority" occurs more often than in any other should have an extraordinary pertinence for a century in which the word "authoritarian" is on so many lips. The central male figure of the drama is one of the most searching studies ever made of the effect of power upon character.

Measure for Measure, like *Troilus and Cressida*, is closely bound to *Hamlet*. It is as if Shakespeare, having exposed in the masterpiece and the plays that culminated in it the futility of revenge as a method of requiting wrong, asked: what then? How, when men fail to keep the peace, shall their quarrels be settled, their misconduct penalized, without resort to personal violence? To that question the all but universal reply of the wiser part of human experience seems to have been: by law. In place of revenge—justice. Instead of personal retaliation—legal adjudication. "A government of laws and not of men": that is the historic answer of those peoples at least who have some freedom. And there in the imposing body of common and statue law to back it up. Trial by jury. Equality before the law. The advance of civilization that these concepts and conquests register cannot be overestimated. Under their spell men are even tempted to the syllogism:

From *The Meaning of Shakespeare*. © 1951 by the University of Chicago. University of Chicago Press, 1951.

> Quarrels are settled by law.
> Wars are just larger quarrels.
> Therefore: wars can be settled by law.

Recent history is little more than the story of the world's disillusionment with regard to this conclusion. The weakness of the syllogism lies in its major premise. "A government of laws and not of men." It sounds august. But there never was, there is not, and there never will be, any such thing. If only laws would construe, administer, and enforce themselves! But until they do, they will rise no nearer justice than the justice in the minds and hearts of their very human agents and instruments. Those with power may sedulously inculcate in subjects the illusion that there is a necessary connection between law and justice as the very cement of the state, without which the political structure would collapse (as well it might); but, philosophically, any mental structure erected on this illusion is built on quicksand. Disillusionment on this subject, if it comes at all, usually comes gradually. We cling to the older and more comforting notion here as we do to infantile ideas of God. When at last we realize that the blessings of the law (which cannot be exaggerated) are due to the wisdom and goodness of man, and its horrors (which also cannot be exaggerated) to his cruelty and greed, we have grasped the fact that law is just an instrument—no more good or bad in itself than the stone we use as a hammer or a missile—and we will never again be guilty of thinking of law and war as opposites, or of confusing peace with the reign of law. Whether the horrors of war are greater or less than the horrors of law may be debated. Shelley, for one, put "legal crime" at the nadir of human baseness. In cowardice, at any rate, it ranks below open violence. *Measure for Measure* records, possibly, Shakespeare's first full disillusionment on this subject.

> It is the law, not I, condemn your brother.

The entire play might be said to have been written just to italicize that lie. The angel-villain tries to hide behind it as behind a shield. So-called civilization tries to do the same. But civilization—as Emerson remarked—crowed too soon.

II

For fourteen years Vienna has suffered from so lax an enforcement of the laws that the very babies have taken to beating their nurses, and a visitor from outside the city might actually

> have seen corruption boil and bubble
> Till it o'er-run the stew: laws for all faults,
> But faults so countenanc'd, that the strong statutes
> Stand like the forfeits in a barber's shop,
> As much in mock as mark.

The ruling Duke decides that, with such a reputation for lenity, he is not the one to rein in a steed that has known no curb. He will delegate his power to a sterner hand and let justice get a fresh start under a new regime. At least, such seems his motive on the surface. But the Duke is a curious character—"the old fantastical Duke of dark corners"—whether born so or made so by the exigencies of Shakespeare's plot. He is as fond of experimenting on human beings and inquiring into their inner workings as a vivisector is of cutting up guinea pigs. And when he retires not for a trip to Poland, as he gives out, but to return, disguised as a Friar, to note the results of his temporary abdication, his motive seems less political and social than psychological. He is really not so much giving up his power as increasing it by retaining it in secret form. The Duke is as introspective as Hamlet, "one that, above all other strifes, contended especially to know himself," and his theatrical instinct also reminds us of the Prince of Denmark, though in his fondness for dazzling his audience he is more like Hal. In spite of his professed love of retirement and hatred of crowds and applause, he is the very reverse of a hermit, and intends (though he doesn't announce the fact in advance and may even be unconscious of it) to burst forth out of the clouds of disguise in full dramatic glory, as he does in the fifth act. His whole plan may be viewed as a sort of play within a play to catch the conscience of his deputy—and of the city. Moreover, he does not intend to miss the performance of his play any more than Hamlet did. The proof that his impulse is melodramatic, or at best psychological, is the fact that he knows at the time he appoints his deputy of a previous act of turpitude on his part. Angelo—for so the deputy is ironically named—deserted the girl to whom he was betrothed when her worldly prospects were wrecked, and slandered her into the bargain to escape the world's censure. He succeeded. His reputation for virtue and austerity is unimpeached. He can be reckoned on to put the screws on all offenders. It is as if the Duke were saying to himself: "Granted that my dispensation has been too lenient; I'll show you what will happen under a paragon of strictness. See how you like it then!" If he had not been more bent on proving his point than on the public welfare, why did he pick out a man whose secret vices he knew? How often have men been given temporary power precisely in order to prove them unworthy of it! Lord Angelo, says the Duke in the first act,

> is precise;
> Stands at a guard with envy; scarce confesses
> That his blood flows, or that his appetite
> Is more to bread than stone: *hence shall we see,*
> *If power change purpose, what our seemers be.*

That last is tolerably explicit. And that there may be no doubt as to what the Duke has in mind, Shakespeare has him again call him "this well-seeming Angelo," when, much later in the play, he reveals his outrageous treatment of Mariana.

III

So Angelo comes to power—ostensibly in association with the kindly and humane but weak-kneed Escalus, who, however, is chiefly a figurehead. The new ruler's hammer comes down first on Claudio, who, under an obsolete blue law, is condemned to death for anticipating the state of marriage with the girl to whom he was betrothed. The judgment is the more reprehensible because the worldly circumstances of the guilty pair demanded a certain concealment, their union was a marriage in fact if not in law, and no question of premeditated infidelity or broken vows was involved. The moral superiority of Claudio to the man who is to judge him is sufficiently pointed. Isabella, Claudio's chaste and virtuous sister, who is about to enter a nunnery, in spite of her reluctance to condone any laxity, intercedes with Angelo on Claudio's behalf. Angelo, at first, will do nothing but repeat "he must die," but as Isabella's beauty mounts with her ardor, the Deputy, who prides himself on being above all such appetites, is suddenly aware of a passion for her, his attitude alters, and he says, with a new sensation at his heart:

> I will bethink me. Come again tomorrow.
> Hark how I'll bribe you;

retorts Isabella, carried beyond discretion by her sense of coming victory.

How! bribe me?

cries Angelo, startled by a word that fits with deadly accuracy a criminal thought he has not dared to confess to himself. We can fairly see him turn on his heel and grow pale.

Ay, with such gifts that heaven shall share with you,

the innocent Isabella replies. But what other Isabella, or what devil within the innocent one, had put that fatally uncharacteristic and inopportune word "bribe" on her tongue? It is one of those single words on which worlds turn that Shakespeare was growing steadily more fond of.

Isabella returns the next day, and Angelo, after hints that produce as little effect as did Edward IV's on Lady Grey, makes the open shameful proposal that the sister herself be the "bribe" to save her brother. Isabella, spurning the infamous suggestion, cries that she will proclaim him to the world if he does not give her an instant pardon for her brother. But when he reminds her that his impeccable reputation will protect him like a wall, she realizes it is true, and goes to report her failure to Claudio and to prepare him for death.

The scene between brother and sister (on which the disguised Duke eavesdrops) is one of the dramatic and poetic pinnacles of Shakespeare, and we scarcely need to except anything even in *Hamlet* when we say that few scenes in his works elicit from different readers more diametrically opposite reactions. Is Isabella to be admired or despised? Some think her almost divine in her virtue; others almost beneath contempt in her self-righteousness. You could fancy the two parties were talking about two different Isabellas. They are. There are two Isabellas.

Hamlet acquaints us with the psychological proximity of heaven and hell. This play goes on to demonstrate that, despite their polarity, the distance between them can be traversed in just about one-fortieth of the time it took Puck to put a girdle round about the earth.

A pendulum is ascending. It reaches the limit gravity will permit and instantly it is descending. A ball is sailing through the air. It touches the bound interposed by a wall and instantly it is sailing in the opposite direction. And even when the reaction is not instantaneous the same principle holds: everything breeds within itself the seed of its contrary. Human passion is no exception to the rule. At the extremity, it too turns the other way around, upside down, or inside out.

"Why, how now, Claudio!" cries Lucio, meeting his friend under arrest and on his way to jail, "whence comes this restraint?"

> CLAUDIO: From too much liberty, my Lucio, liberty:
> As surfeit is the father of much fast,
> So every scope by the immoderate use
> Turns to restraint. Our natures do pursue—
> Like rats that ravin down their proper bane,—
> A thirsty evil, and when we drink we die.

To which Lucio, ever the wit, replies: "I had as lief have the foppery of freedom as the morality of imprisonment." The play is saturated with antitheses like that, and abounds in examples that recall Claudio's rat. There is a woman in it, a bawd and keeper of a brothel, Mistress Overdone, almost the double in marital virtue of Chaucer's Wife of Bath.

> Hath she had any more than one husband?

Escalus inquiries of Pompey, her tapster, and the loyal Pompey proudly replies:

> Nine, sir; Overdone by the last.

Overdone! it might be the name of most of the leading characters of the play. Each of them is too something-or-other. And what they do is likewise overdone. Good and evil get inextricably mixed throughout *Measure for Measure*, for virtue is no exception to the rule, and, pushed to the limit, it turns into vice.

Which brings us back to the two Isabellas.

Whatever it may be to an inveterately twentieth-century mind, the question for Shakespeare does not concern Isabella's rejection of Angelo's advances and her refusal to save her brother at such a price. Any one of his greater heroines—Imogen, Cordelia, Desdemona, Rosalind—in the same position would have decided, instantly, as she did. Who would doubt it? The notion that Isabella is just a self-righteous prude guarding her precious chastity simply will not stand up to the text. Lucio's attitude toward her alone is enough to put it out of court. Her presence can sober this jesting "fantastic" and elicit poetry and sincerity from his loose lips:

> I hold you as a thing ensky'd and sainted,
> By your renouncement an immortal spirit,
> And to be talk'd with in sincerity,
> As with a saint.

Prudes do not produce such effects on libertines and jesters.

The question rather concerns what follows. The sister comes to the brother religiously exalted by a consciousness of the righteousness of what she has done—ever a dangerous aftermath of righteousness. The brother catches something of her uplifted mood.

> CLAUDIO: If I must die,
>   I will encounter darkness as a bride,
>   And hug it in mine arms.
>
>   .   .   .   .
>   There spake my brother,

the sister, thrilled, replies. And there indeed the noblest Claudio did speak, or Shakespeare would never have put such poetry on his lips. But Isabella, whom we interrupted, has instantly gone on:

>   there my father's grave
> Did utter forth a voice. Yes, thou must die.

What a flash of illumination! *Is there a ghost in this play too?*

And when Isabella reveals the terrible price that Angelo has put on his life, Claudio is equal to that too—or he and his sister's spirit are together. Pushed to his limit by that spirit, his instantaneous reaction—it cannot be marked too strongly—is exactly hers:

>   O heavens! it cannot be,

and, again,

>   Thou shalt not do 't.

If it were my life, Isabella cries, I would throw it down like a pin. And she would have *at that moment*, as Claudio perceives:

>   Thanks, dear Isabel.

But Claudio is made of more human stuff than his sister, and, held as she has held him to an extremity of courage and resolution almost beyond his nature, the law of reaction asserts itself and he drops into fear:

> Death is a fearful thing.

And then follows that terrific Dantesque-Miltonic picture of life after death with its "viewless winds" and "thrilling region of thick-ribbed ice" that leaves even Hamlet's similar speculations nowhere—nowhere in appalling power at least. Obscurity made vivid.

> Sweet sister, let me live.

And what does the sweet sister reply?

> O you beast!

Imagine Desdemona saying that! Claudio has said, or done, nothing to deserve such a term. A weak wretch on the threshold of execution, yes. But surely no "beast." What has happened? What always happens. What happened a few seconds before to Claudio himself in another fashion. The overstretched string of Isabella's righteous passion snaps. She has herself dropped from saintliness to beastliness—and projects her own beastliness on her brother. "Isabella—beastly!" her defenders will cry. Why not? There is both beast and saint in every one of us, and whoever will not admit it had better close his Shakespeare once for all, or, rather, open it afresh and learn to change his mind. It is now, not before, that those who have harsh things to say about Isabella may have their innings. Drunk with self-righteousness, she who but a moment ago was offering her life for her brother cries:

> Die, perish! Might but my bending down
> Reprieve thee from thy fate, it should proceed.
> I'll pray a thousand prayers for thy death,
> No word to save thee.

This is religion turned infernal. And it is the worse because of her allusion, in her scene with Angelo, to Christ's atonement:

> Alas, alas!
> Why, all the souls that were were forfeit once;
> And He that might the vantage best have took
> Found out the remedy. How would you be,
> If He, which is the top of judgement, should
> But judge you as you are? O, think on that;
> And mercy then will breathe within your lips,
> Like man new made.

And then, "O you beast!"

What is there to question in this psychology? Is there any human being who cannot confirm it—on however diminished a scale—from his own experience? Who in the midst of making a speech, performing a part, or carrying a point, realizing with delight that it is "coming off," has not paused for a fraction of a second to pat himself on the back, and then—it was indeed all "off" in another sense! The whole thing collapsed, instantly or gradually according to the degree of the complacency.

Commentators have wondered at the pure Isabella's quick acquiescence in the disguised Duke's scheme for having her go back and seem to consent to Angelo's proposal while he arranges to substitute the rejected Mariana, once the Deputy's betrothed, at the rendezvous. You may call the Duke's stratagem vile, shady, or inspired, as you will, and Isabella's reaction to it laudable or damnable. Commendable or not, her conduct is one thing at any rate: credible. It is just the next swing of the pendulum. Conscious, or underconscious, of the fearful injustice she did her brother in that final outburst, she now seeks to set the balance straight. She would not have turned a hand to save him: *therefore*, she will now do anything to save him. Whatever we say, and whatever the Elizabethans said, to the morality of this much debated point, the psychology of it at any rate is sound. Shakespeare's part was done when he showed how a girl made like Isabella would act in those circumstances. And her conduct here coheres perfectly with another bone of contention at the end of the play: her apparent abandonment of getting herself to a nunnery in favor of getting a husband to herself—or at least taking one when offered. Her religious fervor at the outset—with which the ghost of her father plainly had something to do—was "overdone."

And that prospective husband, the Friar—otherwise the Duke! He is tarred with the same brush of excess. He professes to affect retirement and shun publicity. But it is not solitude that he loves. Whatever he was as a ruler, he becomes a moral meddler as a Friar, as intoxicated over the human puppet-show whose strings he is pulling as Angelo is in another way over the moral-social drama of which he is manager. He will lie right and left, and even make innocence suffer cruelly (as in his concealing from Isabella the fact that her brother is not dead), merely for the sake of squeezing the last drops of drama or melodrama from the situation. And we must admit that it *is* a situation indeed, a dozen situations in one, in the last act. *Measure for Measure* has been

widely criticized as an example of Shakespeare's own too great conces-
sion to theatrical effect. The point is in one sense well taken. But the
author very shrewdly shifts the responsibility from himself to the
Duke by making the man who was guilty of the worst offenses of that
sort just the sort of man who would have been guilty of them. The
man who made the great speech beginning:

> Heaven doth with us as we with torches do,
> Not light them for themselves,

had rare insight. It is Shakespeare's own ideal of going forth from
ourselves and shining in, and being reflected from, the lives of others.
But torches can serve the incendiary as well as the illuminator, and
while the Duke did not go quite that far, if we reread the fifth
act—with special attention to his part—the verdict will be: "Overdone
by the last."

The only way to make the Duke morally acceptable is frankly to
take the whole piece as a morality play with the Duke in the role of
God, omniscient and unseen, looking down on the world. As has often
been pointed out, there is one passage that suggests this specifically:

> O my dread lord,

cries the exposed Angelo, when the Duke at last throws off his
disguise,

> I should be guiltier than my guiltiness,
> To think I can be undiscernible,
> *When I perceive your Grace, like power divine,*
> *Hath look'd upon my passes.*

The title of the play—the most "moral" one Shakespeare used–gives
some warrant to the suggestion, as does the general tone of forgiveness
at the end. But if the Duke is God, he is at first a very lax and later a
very interfering God, and both the atmosphere and the characterization
of the play are too intensely realistic to make that way out of the
difficulty entirely satisfactory. If Shakespeare wants us to take it so, the
execution of his intention is not especially successful. But we may at
any rate say there is a morality play lurking behind *Measure for Measure.*

IV

And this brings us to the apex of the triangle, or the pyramid,

Angelo, for the illumination of whom almost everything in the play seems expressly inserted.

Angelo is one of the clearest demonstrations in literature of the intoxicating nature of power as such. Power means unbounded opportunity, and opportunity acts on the criminal potentialities in man as gravitation does on an apple. Shakespeare wrote his *Rape of Lucrece* around this theme (and came back to it in *Macbeth*), and the stanzas on Opportunity in that poem are the best of glosses on *Measure for Measure*, such lines, to cull out just a few, as

> O Opportunity, thy guilt is great!
>
> . . . .
>
> Thou sett'st the wolf where he the lamb may get
>
> . . . .
>
> And in thy shady cell, where none may spy him,
>
> . . . .
>
> Sits Sin, to seize the souls that wander by him
>
> . . . .
>
> Thou blow'st the fire when temperance is thaw'd
>
> . . . .
>
> Thou foul abettor! thou notorious bawd!

This is why power as such is so often synonymous with crime. "Power as such," said Emerson, "is not known to the angels." But it was known to Angelo.

Angelo, in spite of his treatment of his betrothed, Mariana, was not an intentional villain or tyrant. His affinities are not with Pandulph and Richard III, but with Edward IV and Claudius. His soliloquy, on his knees,

> When I would pray and think, I think and pray
> To several subjects. Heaven hath my empty words,

looks back to Hamlet's uncle, as his

> Would yet he had liv'd!

when he supposes Claudio is dead at his command looks forward to Macbeth. But his case is in a way worse than theirs, for, supposing himself a mountain of virtue, when the temptation—and with it a sensation he has never experienced—comes, he rolls almost instantly into the abyss. Spiritual pride erects no defenses.

> ANGELO: I have begun,
>   And now I give my sensual race the rein.

He loathes himself:

> The tempter or the tempted, who sins most?
> Ha!
> Not she; nor doth she tempt: but it is I
> That, lying by the violet in the sun,
> Do as the carrion does, . . . *Most dangerous*
> *Is that temptation that doth goad us on*
> *To sin in loving virtue.*

In loving Isabella, he thinks he means. But how much profounder the second construction that the sentence bears, which makes it embrace both intending violator and intended victim! Though poles apart, the virtuous maid and the respected head of the state are here identical. Their vulnerable spot is the same: the sin of loving their own virtue.

There are few passages in Shakespeare that give a more inescapable impression of coming from the poet himself than Isabella's great speech to Angelo on power. It is the speech perhaps above any other in his works that seems written to the twentieth century and that the twentieth century should know by heart. The spectacle of

> man, proud man,
>   Dress'd in a little brief authority,

"like an angry ape" playing "fantastic tricks before high heaven" made Shakespeare as well as the angels weep. But her words recoil too perfectly on Isabella's own head not to make them also perfectly in character:

> Merciful Heaven!
> Thou rather with thy sharp and sulphurous bolt
> Split'st the unwedgeable and gnarled oak
> Than the soft myrtle.

This shaft is aimed at the man who would make the soft Claudio a public example of the moral austerity of his regime. But how about Isabella herself, who is shortly to launch thunderbolts against the same weakling in the scene where she calls him beast?—not to mention what she is doing at the moment, for Angelo in strength is nearer the myrtle than the oak he considers himself. *Tu quoque!* Shakespeare perceives

that spiritual power is quite as open to abuse as political power. The
sheer theatrical effectiveness of this astonishing scene can easily blind
us to the tangle of moral ironies and boomerangs it involves. This
retiring girl, who had fairly to be pushed into the encounter by Lucio,
finally standing up with audacity to the first man of the state is
thrilling drama. But unfortunately Isabella gets an inkling of that fact
herself.

> Go to your bosom,

she cautions Angelo,

> Knock there, and ask your heart what it doth know
> That's like my brother's fault.

If only she could have said those lines to herself, substituting for the
last one,

> That's like this man's offence,

she never would have let slip from her lips that fatal word that ties
some unplumbed sensual element in her own nature to the very corruption of justice and virtue she is condemning.

But Angelo's blackest act is not his sin of sensuality against
Isabella, which he commits in wish and as he thinks in fact. Nor is it
even the prostitution of his office that that involves. It is his acceptance of Isabella's sacrifice of herself and his then sending Claudio to
death nevertheless. This final infamy—completed in intention though
defeated in fact—ranks with John of Lancaster's treachery to the rebels
in *Henry IV*. Nothing worse need be said of it than that.

> Alack! when once our grace we have forgot,
> Nothing goes right,

Angelo cries, in anguish at what he has done. He might just as well
have said,

> Alack! When once our power is unbounded,
> Nothing goes right,

for his are the typical sins and crimes of unlimited authority.
"Power is poison."
What power is has never been more tersely summed up than in
those three words of Henry Adams in the section of the *Education* in

which he analyzes its effect on presidents of the United States, as he had observed it in Washington.

> Power is poison. Its effect on Presidents had been always tragic, chiefly as an almost insane excitement at first, and a worse reaction afterwards; but also because no mind is so well balanced as to bear the strain of seizing unlimited force without habit or knowledge of it; and finding it disputed with him by hungry packs of wolves and hounds whose lives depend on snatching the carrion. . . . *The effect of unlimited power on limited mind is worth noting in Presidents because it must represent the same process in society, and the power of self-control must have limit somewhere in face of the control of the infinite.*

Shakespeare was saying precisely that, I think, in *Measure for Measure.* If concentration of authority in time of "peace" can let loose such demons of Opportunity in those who possess power, and transform their subjects either into pelting petty officers, hungry packs of wolves and hounds, or into their victims, what will the same thing do in time of war? In "peace" such unadulterated authority is at least not "necessary." It is the crowning infamy of war that it does make it essential. Victory demands efficiency, and efficiency calls for undisputed unity of command. War is authority—overdone.

V

The underplot of this play is unsavory. But of its kind it is a masterpiece of the first order, both in itself and in its integration with the main plot and its themes. Mistress Overdone, the keeper of a Viennese brothel, Abhorson, the executioner in a Viennese prison, and Barnardine, a condemned murderer, may be said to be its symbolic triad. A prison is presumably a place where Justice is done. Pompey, Mistress Overdone's tapster, is struck rather by its resemblance to his employer's establishment.

"I am as well acquainted here as I was in our house of profession: one would think it were Mistress Overdone's own house, for here be many of her old customers. First, here's young Master Rash" and foregoing acquaintance with the rest of the inmates whom Pompey goes on to introduce, we are sent back in astonished recognition, by that name "Master Rash," to Hamlet (and his "prais'd be rashness") who first made known to us the idea that the world is a prison. This play carries Hamlet's analogy a step further, and continually suggests the resemblance of the main world, not so much to a prison—though it is that too—as to a house of ill fame, where men and women sell their honors in a dozen senses.

Lucio, for instance, mentions "the sanctimonious pirate, that went to sea with the Ten Commandments, but scraped one out of the table." If this is not an oblique, if a bit blunt, hit at Angelo (on Shakespeare's part of course, not Lucio's), then a cap that fits should never be put on. It was "Thou shalt not steal," of course, that the pirate scraped out. We know which one of the ten Angelo eliminated, if, indeed, it was not half-a-dozen of them. It would be interesting, taking Lucio's hint, to run through the cast and ask which and how many of the commandments each character discarded. Isabella certainly could close her eyes to the first one. But without taking time for the experiment, one thing is certain. There would be no perfect scores—either way. The man in ermine in this play casts wanton eyes on the same woman whom the libertine looks on as a saint. That is typical of almost everything in it.

" 'Twas never merry world," declares Pompey, comparing his profession with a more respectable one, "since, òf two usuries, the merriest was put down, and the worser allowed by order of law a furred gown to keep him warm; and furred with fox and lambskins too, to signify that craft, being richer than innocency, stands for the facing." This might be dismissed as the irresponsible chatter of the barroom, did not the main plot so dreadfully confirm it and Angelo himself confess it in soliloquy:

> Thieves for their robbery have authority
> When judges steal themselves.

If it will help any ultramodern person to understand Pompey's "usuries," read "rackets" in their place.

When the Provost tells this same Pompey, then in prison, that he may earn his freedom if he will act as assistant to the executioner, Shakespeare gives us another of his deadly parallels between the world of law and the world of lawbreakers. Pompey jumps at the chance: "Sir, I have been an unlawful bawd time out of mind; but yet I will be content to be a lawful hangman." But Abhorson, who is proud of his calling, is scandalized at the suggestion: "A bawd, sir? Fie upon him! he will discredit our mystery." To which the Provost replies: "A feather will turn the scale." (Between being bawd and executioner, he means, of course.) As to what Shakespeare thought, we get a hint when we remember the Duke's tribute:

> This is a gentle Provost: seldom when
> The steeled gaoler is the friend of men.

So recklessly does Shakespeare go on heaping up analogies between persons and things of low and those of high estate that when Elbow, the Constable, who must have been Dogberry's cousin, brings Froth and Pompey before Angelo and Escalus in judicial session, and introduces his prisoners as "two notorious benefactors," we begin to wonder, in the general topsy-turvydom, whether there may not be relative truth in his malapropism. At any rate, the upperworld characters are guilty of far worse moral and mental, if not verbal, confusions. "Which is the wiser here," asks Escalus, "Justice or Iniquity?"

> And you shall have your bosom on this wretch,

cries the disguised Duke to Isabella, when Angelo's infamy becomes known to him,

> Grace of the Duke, revenges to your heart,
> And general honour.

An odd idea of honor for a supposed Friar to impart to a prospective nun: the time-worn notion that it consists in having all your old scores settled. And when he hears that "a most notorious pirate" has just died in prison of a fever, thus supplying a head that can be sent to Angelo in place of Claudio's, he exclaims:

> O, 'tis an accident that Heaven provides!

—an equally odd idea of heaven. But he far exceeds these lapses. At the end of the play, in an atmosphere of general pardon, Lucio, who—unwittingly but not unwittily—has abused the Duke to his face when disguised as a Friar, does not escape. The Duke orders him married to the mother of his illegitimate child, and, the ceremony over, whipped and hanged. "I beseech your Highness," Lucio protests, "do not marry me to a whore." And the Duke relents to the extent of remitting the last two but not the first of the three penalties.

The emphasis on this incident at the very end brings to mind the moment when Lucio pulls off the Duke's hood:

DUKE: Thou art the first knave that e'er mad'st a Duke . . .
    Come hither, Mariana.
    Say, wast thou e'er contracted to this woman?
ANGELO: I was, my lord.
DUKE: Go take her hence, and marry her instantly.

Poor Mariana's willingness, in contrast with Lucio, to marry *her* "knave" makes the parallelism more rather than less pointed.

Measure for Measure—once one gives the underplot its due—fairly bristles with disconcerting analogies and moral paradoxes like this last one. Only a hopelessly complacent person will not be challenged by it. And whoever will be honest with himself will confess, I believe, to a strange cumulative effect that it produces. Barring Escalus and the Provost, who are put in to show that not all judges are harsh nor all jailers hardhearted, we are more in love in the end with the disreputable than with the reputable characters. Overworld and underworld threaten to change places.

Whether *Measure for Measure* was a favorite play of Samuel Butler's I do not know. It ought to have been. In it Shakespeare certainly proves himself a good Butlerian, an adherent to the principle that "every proposition has got a skeleton in its cupboard." Many entries in the *Note-Books* might have been composed to illuminate Shakespeare's play:

> God is not so white as he is painted, and he gets on better with the Devil than people think. The Devil is too useful for him to wish him ill and, in like manner, half the Devil's trade would be at an end should any great mishap bring God well down in the world. . . . The conception of them as the one absolutely void of evil and the other of good is a vulgar notion taken from science whose priests have ever sought to get every idea and every substance pure of all alloy.
>
> God and the Devil are about as four to three. There is enough preponderance of God to make it far safer to be on his side than on the Devil's, but the excess is not so great as his professional *claqueurs* pretend it is.

What is this but the repentant Angelo's

> Let's write good angel on the devil's horn,

slightly expanded?

Quite in conformity with Butler's dicta, I am not sure that honest readers do not find Barnardine, the condemned murderer, the most delectable character in *Measure for Measure*—he who for God knows how long has defied the efforts of the prison authorities to execute him. We like him so well that we do not wish to inquire too curiously into his past. For my part, I am certain the murder he did—if he really did it—was an eminently good-natured one. "Thank you kindly for your attention," he says in effect, when they come to hale him to the gallows, "but I simply cannot be a party to any such proceeding. I am too busy—sleeping." Let him sleep. Let anyone sleep to his heart's content who puts to rout one Abhorson. He has earned his nap.

Like Falstaff, Barnardine tempts the imagination to play around him. No higher tribute can be paid to a character in a play, as none can to a person in life. The fascination he has for us—he, and, in less degree, the rest of the underworld of which he is a member—is partly because these men and women, being sinners, have some tolerance for sin. And some humor, which comes to much the same thing. *Judge not*: they come vastly nearer obeying that injunction (of which *Measure for Measure* sometimes seems a mere amplification) than do their betters. Never will anyone say of them as Escalus said of Angelo: "my brother justice have I found so severe, that he hath forced me to tell him he is indeed Justice." They are not forever riding the moral high horse. They make no pretensions. They mind their own business, bad as it is, instead of telling, or compelling, other people to mind *theirs* or to act in *their* way. It is a relief to find somebody of whom that is true. "Our house of profession." No, Pompey is wrong. It is not the establishment to which he is bawd and tapster, but the main world, that better deserves that name. For everybody with power—save a few Abraham Lincolns—is, *ipso facto*, professing and pretending all day long. "I am convinced, almost instinctively," says Stendhal, "that as soon as he opens his mouth every man in power begins to lie, and so much the more when he writes." It is a strong statement, and Shakespeare would certainly have inserted an "almost" in his version of it, but there are his works, from the history plays on, to show his substantial agreement with it. Why does Authority always lie? Because it perpetuates itself by lies and thereby saves itself from the trouble of crude force: costumes and parades for the childish, decorations and degrees for the vain and envious, positions for the ambitious, propaganda for the docile and gullible, orders for the goosesteppers, fine words (like "loyalty" and "co-operation") for the foolishly unselfish—to distract, to extort awe, to flatter and gratify inferiority, as the case may be. Dr. Johnson ought to have amended his famous saying. Patriotism is only one of the last refuges of a scoundrel.

Angelo and the Duke, if anyone, ought to know, and in their hearts they agree exactly. Hear them in soliloquy. The identity is not accidental.

> ANGELO: O place, O form,
> How often dost thou with thy case, thy habit,
> Wrench awe from fools and tie the wiser souls
> To thy false seeming!
> DUKE: O place and greatness! millions of false eyes
> Are stuck upon thee. Volumes of report
> Run with these false and most contrarious quests
> Upon thy doings; thousand escapes of wit
> Make thee the father of their idle dream
> And rack thee in their fancies.

The effect of power on those who do not possess it but wish that they did, Shakespeare concludes, is scarcely better than on those who do.

And here in the deepest reason—is it not?—why we prefer the "populace" in this play to the powers-that-be. The vices of the two ends of "society" turn out under examination to be much alike. But the lower stratum has one virtue to which the possessors and pursuers of power, for all their pretensions, cannot pretend: namely, lack of pretension. Here is a genuine basis for envying the dispossessed. Revolutions by the downtrodden, abortive or successful, to regain their share of power have occurred throughout history. The world awaits a revolution by the powerful to gain relief from the insincerities to which their privileges and position forever condemn them. Thoreau staged a one-man revolution based on a kindred principle. If this is what it implies, *Measure for Measure* may yet be banned by the authorities. . . . But no! it is as safe as the music of Beethoven. "The authorities" will never understand it.

VI

If we do not want a world presided over by a thundering Jove— this play seems to say—and under him a million pelting petty officers and their understudies, and under *them* millions of their victims, we must renounce Power as our god—Power and all his ways. And not just in the political and military worlds, where the evils of autocracy with its inevitable bureaucracy of fawning yes-men, while obvious to all but autocratic or servile eyes, may be more or less "necessary." It is the more insidiously personal bondages to power that should concern us first. Revolution against authority—as Isabella, for all her great speech, did not perceive, and as Barnardine did—begins at home. Let men in sufficient numbers turn into Barnardines, who want to run no one else but will not *be* run by anyone, even to the gallows, and what would be left for the pelting petty officers, and finally for Jove himself, but to follow suit? There would be a revolution indeed. The more we meditate on Barnardine the more he acquires the character of a vast symbol, the key perhaps to all our troubles. Granted, with Hamlet, that the world is a prison. We need not despair with Hamlet. We may growl rather with Barnardine at all intruders on our daydreams, and learn with him that even in a prison life may be lived—independently. Why wait, as modern gospels preach, until we are out of prison before beginning to live? "Now is a time."

Approximately three hundred years before the twentieth century, *Measure for Measure* made clear the truths that it has taken two world wars to burn into the consciousness of our own generation: that Power lives by Authority and that Authority is always backed by two things, the physical force that tears bodies and the mental violence that mutilates brains:

> In every cry of every Man,
> In every Infant's cry of fear,
> In every voice, in every ban,
> The mind-forg'd manacles I hear.

The two—dynamite and propaganda, to use modern terms—are always found together. "By skilful and sustained propaganda," said Hitler, "an entire people can be made to see even heaven as hell and the most miserable life as paradise." Where there is an Angelo on the bench, there will always be an Abhorson in the cellar. And how well Shakespeare liked Abhorson, his name proclaims.

> O, it is excellent
> To have a giant's strength; but it is tyrannous
> To use it like a giant.
> . . . .
> Could great men thunder

As Jove himself does, Jove would ne'er be quiet;
For every pelting, petty officer
Would use his heaven for thunder,
Nothing but thunder! Merciful Heaven!
Thou rather with thy sharp and sulphurous bolt
Split'st the unwedgeable and gnarled oak
Than the soft myrtle; but man, proud man,
Dress'd in a little brief authority,
Most ignorant of what he's most assur'd,
His glassy essence, like an angry ape,
Plays such fantastic tricks before high heaven
As make the angels weep; who, with our spleens,
Would all themselves laugh mortal.

Measure for Measure

A. P. Rossiter

> Oh, wearisome condition of Humanity!
> Born under one law, to another bound;
> Vainly begot, and yet forbidden vanity;
> Created sick, commanded to be sound;
> What meaneth Nature by these diverse laws?
> Passion and Reason, self-division's cause.
>
> Is it the mark or majesty of power
> To make offences that it may forgive?
> Nature herself doth her own self deflower
> To hate those errors she herself doth give.
> But how should man think what he may not do,
> If Nature did not fail, and punish too?
>
> Tyrant to others, to herself unjust,
> Only commands things difficult and hard.
> Forbids us all things which it knows we lust,
> Makes easy pains, impossible reward.
> If Nature did not take delight in blood,
> She would have made more easy ways to good.
>
> We that are bound by vows and by promotion,
> With pomp of holy sacrifice and rites,
> To lead belief in good and still devotion,
> To preach of heaven's wonders and delights;
> Yet when each of us in his own heart looks,
> He finds the God there far unlike his books.
>
> FULKE GREVILLE, LORD BROOKE

UNDERSHAFT: You have learnt something. That always feels, at first, as if you had *lost* something.

> BERNARD SHAW, *Major Barbara*

From *Angel with Horns: Fifteen Lectures on Shakespeare*, edited by Graham Storey. © 1961 by Longman, Green & Co., Ltd. Theatre Art Books, 1961.

I have presented tragicomedy as an inquisition into human nature and humanism; and that implies an inquiry into what controls human nature: into "institutions" such as the principles of order, the essences of honour or virtue, etc. I have insisted that these inquiries are "sceptical," in the sense of relying on empirical observation, not on *a priori* hypotheses: in the same way that Donne's inquiries into love are empirical—and sceptical.

In drama, this means investigating (in the frame of a play) things as they are, as distinct from "seemings"; and as deceit is human, this means the unmasking of Man. I have (I hope) firmly rejected the term "cynical" for that. Cynics do not ask questions: they know the answers. "Pessimistic" I refuse to argue about: beyond saying that to call the empirical observation of Man (or anything else) "pessimistic" is only the emotive expression of a preference for some kind of delusion.

Tragicomedy found this inquisitorial field through the critical use of the comic in "serious" plots: "serious" (rather than "tragic"), because in them the sceptical contemplation of Man checks approach to tragic greatness, even if the pseudo-hero is not presented as too pinched by *circumstance* to have the necessary degree of freedom. In the pseudo-heroes Troilus and Bertram, a critical and intellectual detachment checks or denies sympathy; and that is what makes their plays inquisitions. Jonson's intellectual-critical comedies differ only in degree.

Expert inquisitors manipulate circumstances so that the truth is extracted from men undistorted. They do it by playing on weaknesses; and all men are weak before unknowns. In dramatic inquisitions, highly improbable circumstances are used (the Trojan War is a fantastic one, and Bertram's a fairy-tale marriage); but out of these "possible improbabilities" are wrung implications about human fundamentals: about action, passion, pride, honour, love, justice. This gives the plays the air of being highly developed Moralities: with this difference, that the accepted *code* itself may be on trial. Order is, I think, in *Troilus and Cressida*; in *Measure for Measure* nobody questions that justice is on trial. In *All's Well [That Ends Well]*, it is virtue, mainly examined as masculine honour. How all these intertwist is shown by a passage in Montaigne which Shakespeare used in *All's Well*:

> We taste nothing purely. . . . When I religiously confess
> myself unto myself, I find the best good I have hath some
> vicious taint . . . if Plato in his purest virtue had listened to
> it . . . he would have heard therein some harsh tune, of

human mixture, but an obscure tune, and only sensible to himself. . . . Man all in all is but a botching and party-coloured work. The very Laws of Justice, can not subsist without some commixture of Injustice.

Now sex is a human fundamental: it is also a theme where the web of life is a highly mingled yarn, and man most plainly a "botching and party-coloured work," if you look clear-sightedly and empirically at all the facts. But as it is a theme too on which human hypocrisy (self-defensive masking) is highly developed, the inquisitor needs ingenuity in manipulating his circumstances. It would be hard to devise a more shrewdly searching situation than one in which a nun and a pimp comment on an unwanted pregnancy; yet Shakespeare's ingenuity adds to the discussion-group a severely chaste male Puritan and a gentlemanly whoremonger, a good-natured worldly magistrate and the expectant father. That is only one aspect of *Measure for Measure*: yet one in which human nature must inevitably give itself away a lot, in the opinion that each of the six expresses. (There is something almost prophetic in staging the play in Freud's own city of Vienna.)

The situation is twisted tighter still by making the sex-mishap truly a matter of life and death: through a law which is completely Gilbertian. Like the "wise Mikado (virtuous man)," the Duke is

> Resolved to try
> A plan whereby
> Young men might best be steadied.
> So he decreed, in words succinct,
> That all who flirted, leered or winked
> (Unless connubially linked),
> Should forthwith be beheaded.

—only, *he* has an old dead-letter law which can be recalled to operation. Angelo's task is to do this: to make men chaste by act of Parliament; and this brings in not only the unchaste Claudio, but the brothel-world as well. To them too

> This stern decree, you'll understand
> Caused wide dismay.

The point of my analogy is that, unless the persons are presented very realistically, the Gilbertian absurdity will make the whole thing a fantasy; and that this kind of flippant badinage on sex *is* a normal (if also hypocritically denied) human attitude towards "getting into trouble." You may say "not normal to *me*": I congratulate you. For others (who do not see life with that clear-eyed empiricism), I may add that such flippancy is partly a defence-reaction—"denying the importunity of the blood" by making sex a base jest—and partly the index of a potential or real hardness of sensibility. Lucio and his fellow-gentlemen stand for both. They are a chorus of *je m'en fiche*, the voices of shallowness of mind and feeling; yet their jesting has a serious implication, since all turns on the incongruity of men's dignified pretensions and their animal behaviour; and on the latter's usual consequences: sexual scandal and venereal disease (as a kind of cruel practical joke which makes the sufferer ridiculous). Lucio is an entirely human being: if very low, he is also very funny. And though he "stands for" sex intellectualized as witty smuttiness, stripped of emotion and therefore debased, he is a mingled yarn; for there are touches in him of good sense in a "low" mind which is denied to his betters. "Why, what a ruthless thing is this in him, for the rebellion of a codpiece to take away the life of a man!" (3.2.106); and (earlier in the same scene): "but it is impossible to extirp it quite, Friar, till eating and drinking be put down." The humane (and respectable) Provost agrees: "All sects, all ages, smack of this vice; and he / To die for't!" (2.2.5).

The comic part of the play ("very natural and pleasing": Johnson!) acts as a commentary on the difficulty of applying *law* (a reasoned thing) to matters of *instinct*. It supports the serious part, which results in a damaging analysis of the shortcomings of law and justice as social institutions. It also has its own farcical sidelight to throw on law in the persons of its officers (Elbow *versus* Pompey). And it presents aspects of sex which reflect on the sexual side of the main plot: so that lust—like law—is subjected to an inquisitorial cross-questioning. The worlds of Mrs. Overdone and Pompey, of Claudio and Julietta, and of Isabella and Angelo, all meet—in *prison*. One might say, "In human bondage" (in the sense in which Somerset Maugham took the title from Spinoza).

Lust is *disorder* and *confusion* of good and bad. I consider that the Duke's absconding from office must be taken as symbolic shorthand for the abrogation of "degree" and order. He is not a personification of the gospel ethic (Wilson Knight); nor a peripatetic Providence performing a "controlled experiment" (F. R. Leavis); much less "the Incarnate Lord" in an allegory of the Atonement (R. W. Battenhouse). He is not a character who moves in the same plane as the rest (the Arden editor went wildly astray here), and he does "stand for" government and "the Prince's duty" (E. M. Pope) in the overall pattern; though he is a shadowy figure, and his speech "Be absolute for death" is apart from the rest.

What follows the Duke's abrogation of his office is the exposure of a corrupted world. "What Tiresias *sees*, in fact, is the substance of the poem," Eliot wrote of *The Waste Land*. What the Duke sees is *inversion*, topsyturveydom. The images in

> And liberty plucks justice by the nose;
> The baby beats the nurse, and quite athwart
> Goes all decorum
>
> (1.3.29–31)

are not only paralleled by Ulysses and by Timon: they belong to a European tradition—pictorial and literary—to the traditional figure of *Die Verkehrte Welt, Le Monde Renversé,* the Inverted World. (Breugel painted it in his *Flemish Proverbs*. The *topoi* are traced by E. R. Curtius from Virgil, *Ecl.*,8.53f.; and Breugel's picture shows humanity doing the opposite of all that traditional wisdom—crystallized in *Proverbs*—says it should or should not do). I mention this, because (1) Peter Brook's production at Stratford in 1950 appositely dressed the "low life" Flemishly and from Breugel: 1.2. really proclaimed the vices. (2) This inversion-figure does symbolize the essential clash or disharmony in *Measure for Measure*: that things and people, "realistically" seen and staged, indeed are like that (odd as they look); but by all the rights of things, they should not be. For example, the vice beneath the judge's robe; the humanity of the Overdones and Pompeys—a sanity which is pearls in mud. The inverted world is the subject of "Tir'd with all these, for restful death I cry" (Sonnet 66). It is the subject too of the "cryptic" sentences of the Duke at 3.2.208:

ESCALUS: What news abroad i' th' world?

DUKE: None, but that there is so great a fever on goodness that the dissolution of it must cure it. Novelty is only in request; and, as it is, as dangerous to be aged in any kind of course as it is virtuous to be constant in any undertaking. . . . Much upon this riddle runs the wisdom of the world.

With the development of the Angelo plot, this "disorder" theme enwraps the whole. The Puritan has been specifically appointed Deputy to clean up a very dirty city; but when Claudio's life is in his hands and his sister comes to plead for it, lust determines him to rape the nun, by blackmail. The conflict of sex and law, which *is* Vienna, erupts in him too—and law or justice itself becomes a mask:

> O place, O form,
> How often dost thou with thy case, thy habit,
> Wrench awe from fools, and tie the wiser souls
> To thy false seeming!
>
> (2.4.12–15)

The Duke and Isabella express the same idea: "the demigod Authority" is a *seeming* where

> Degree being vizarded,
> Th' unworthiest shows as fairly in the mask.
>
> (*Troilus and Cressida,* 1.3.83–84)

It is not only his robe which masks Angelo. "Ha! little honour to be much believ'd," Isabella cries when he has revealed his "most pernicious purpose." Seeming, seeming!" But he meets her threat to expose him by showing her his other mask—his chilly reputation: "my unsoil'd name, th' austereness of my life." Hardness of that *will* which is lust defeats her: just as the other hardness of will—a narrow self-righteousness—had turned aside the appeal of the tolerant, worldly wise Escalus:

> Ay, but yet
> Let us be keen, and rather cut a little
> Than fall and bruise to death.
>
> (2.1.5f.)

But Isabella calls out for Christian charity, and truly speaks as "a thing enskied and sainted":

> Why, all the souls that were were forfeit once;
> And He that might the vantage best have took
> Found out the remedy. How would you be
> If He, which is the top of judgment, should
> But judge you as you are?
>
> (2.2.73–77)

> Go to your bosom,
> Knock there, and ask your heart what it doth know
> That's like my brother's fault.
>
> (2.2.136–38)

There is a terrible irony here: he could answer nothing at the very moment when her beauty, her impassioned sense, had struck home to his heart. The two scenes with Isabella are unlike anything else in Shakespeare, and few, few indeed retain such power on the modern stage.

But exactly there—at the end of act 2—the difficulties begin: with the soliloquy which contains "More than our brother is our chastity." This and the subsequent hardness towards the terrified Claudio, who has come to see a dreadful ray of hope, turn some critical ink to gall at Isabella's expense. Other critics cling to her saintliness as if it were their own. Sir Arthur Quiller-Couch calls the character inconsistent; Dr. Tillyard brings in Whetstone to explain. L. C. Knights calls it "ambiguity"; and Dr. Leavis says "why assume it must be "either or?"—"chaste serenity" or self-regarding puritanism." These critical contradictions are quite needless if you can entertain the concept of *ambivalence*. Isabella is a dramatic parallel to Angelo untempted. In both, the higher nature (of a Christian kind: Pauline Christianity) is taken too high; and by being too far from instinctive sympathy, approaches the unnatural. Lucio's very remarkable "fertility" speech (1.4.39–44) is "implied criticism" (F. R. Leavis) of Christian tradition. The apparent intention was to show Isabella first as the nun-elect (Johnson); then as exemplifying Langland's "Chastity without Charity is chained in hell"; and, finally, as released—by a real conversion—to magnanimity. But the graph we read in the play is quite incoherent; hence the commentators' interpolations. They call the process "interpretative criticism": in Bradley they damn it as invention (which it often is).

But "More than our brother is our chastity" need trouble no one. The line makes sense—whatever Quiller-Couch, Una Ellis-Fermor and others may say—if you see that Isabella is just as terrified as Claudio is, and with an analogous cry of the reluctant flesh. As he fears death, so she fears the unknown violence and violation of lust (". . . and go we know not where; / To lie . . . to rot . . . or to be worse than worst / Of those that lawless and incertain thought / Imagine howling.") Hence her hysteria as she screams at Claudio "O you beast! O faithless coward! O

dishonest wretch! . . . Die; perish." It makes "More than our brother
. . ." something very different from that tight-lipped, resolved, hard-
principled, priggish utterance which the angry chastisers of Isabella
apparently hear. Scared souls are small souls; and as she leaves Angelo,
Isabella's soul is scared—to a tiny rod of iron principle which is all she
can think. She is beyond despair. "Who would believe me?" What
irony there is in that line! There is not a soul in Vienna who would *not*,
so far as we can judge: not even the eavesdropping Duke, who never
for a moment believes what he tells Claudio—that it is only Angelo's
"practice" or a try-on to put her to the test, not meant.

Again:

> had he twenty heads to tender down
> On twenty bloody blocks, he'd yield them up
> Before his sister should her body stoop
> To such abhorr'd pollution.

The hyperbole reveals her real doubts of Claudio: but she dare not
think, dare not calculate; and so entertains the notion of this obliging
hydra, rather than realize now a Claudio with only *one* head; for that
way lies despair too.

Her fury at Claudio is the fury we feel at people made the centre
of self-indulgent fantasy, when we find them mere humans. I am not
"against" Isabella: it is a very painful emotion. But brother and sister
are of one family in lacking imagination (sympathetic insight); or their
circumstances make them appear akin. And they are akin in selfishness;
or in self-preservation, without insight into the cost—to another. Hence
there is a hollowness in Isabella's avowal that she would "strip myself
to death as to a bed": she is too ready for the rhetorical sacrifice which
has not been asked of her. "I would sooner die" is rhetoric unless you
achieve your aim by dying; and her aim is to save Claudio's life—to
which her readiness to be stripped and whipped does not contribute.
But, again, she is scared there; and to take the lines as a programme
("greater love hath no man") is to misread them.

But Isabella does not *end* as "small-souled." Her plea for Angelo
has a sufficient magnanimity, though Shakespeare has not built up to
it, and it can be taken several ways. (1) We can see her speech as
consistent with "More than our brother": chastity has not been lost,
and if Claudio has—well, "My brother had but justice," he deserved to
die, and was the minor issue. On this view, Isabella is presumably a
"realist"? (2) "Till he did look on me" opens awkward doors. "I did

all this wickedness for you" is a formula of seduction for a woman; and "this man wanted *me*" is surely not a weak undermining—when there is no chance of his proceeding further? Is Isabella then mere woman? (3) She is—or ought to be—in love with the Friar-Duke; and therefore feels for Mariana. And what is the good of revenge *now*? (4) "I partly think / A due sincerity govern'd his deeds" marks her theoretical sympathy with the snow-broth frenzy. The official half of Angelo is just such a hard man on lechery as she would admire, support, and aid ("There is a vice that most I do abhor"). She is still intellectually a Puritan.

Shakespeare's fault lies in giving Isabella no transitions. She ought to require some overpersuading before she permits Mariana to do rather more than Julietta had done by way of risking her soul. (Julietta is "fast" Claudio's wife; Angelo has rejected Mariana—and might refuse to marry her. She would then be—casuistically, I suppose, and legally, without doubt—worse off than the seduced Isabella: for Isabella would have submitted to Angelo without consent of the will, and presumably without falling into desire—lust—at all. But what Shakespeare thought here is anybody's guess.) Again, her plea for Angelo comes too suddenly, too like a Beaumont and Fletcher switchover—without *thought*. Yet she is a thinking woman: hence intellectuals fall for her—as Angelo did ("She speaks, and 'tis / Such sense that my sense breeds with it": 2.2.141–42). But though she twice needs to show hard thinking, and is entirely the woman for it, Shakespeare does not let her open her mind to us. This is worse than her silence for over eighty lines at the end of the play, before she declines coyly into the ex-Friar's bosom.

"Chastity" some critics call her: but what would St. Paul have to say to this? Chastity should be in no such inner combustion as to fly from fire even to ducal arms. And she does it with no dramatic preparation either, making it hard on both actress and critics. The "conventional" comedy ending is a weak plea. There is no need for either Duke or cloistress to marry to end the play—unless we are being pushed up to an allegorical plane, which is "unconformable" with the realism and psychology of acts 1–3. Moreover, Shakespeare plots points on Isabella's curve which require a true conversion. At 4.3.131–33 the Friar offers her revenge on Angelo:

> And you shall have your bosom on this wretch,
> Grace of the Duke, revenges to your heart,
> And general honour.

Revenges do not go with the enskied and sainted object of the "Christian" critics; and we equivocate much if, quoting Prospero or Scripture, we say that "revenges" here means the opposite.

It is not only Isabella's character which is "double." The whole play is full of equivocal speeches, of a kind where there is no resolving the ambiguities, since both meanings "belong" in the play frame. Sometimes quite opposite value judgments are involved:

> CLAUDIO: Fellow, why dost thou show me thus to th' world?
> Bear me to prison, where I am committed. . . .
> Thus can the demigod Authority
> Make us pay down for our offence by weight
> The words of heaven: on whom it will, it will;
> On whom it will not, so; yet still 'tis just.
>
> (1.2.110ff.)

He alludes to Rom. 9:18: "Therefore hath he mercy on whom he will have mercy, and whom he will he hardeneth." But "yet still 'tis just" can equally be Claudio's bitter comment that Authority can order these needless shames once you are in its hands: and "it is all called *just*." No actor can play contrite resignation and angry bitterness at once.

This same quality appears in the oddly frequent use of *hendiadys* (seen in *Troilus and Cressida* and *Hamlet* too): e.g., "leaven'd and prepared choice" (1.1.52); "the fault and glimpse of newness" (1.2.151); "a prone and speechless dialect" (1.2.176); "rebate and blunt his natural edge" (1.4.60); "nicety and prolixious blushes" (2.4.162); "abominable and beastly touches" (3.2.21); "lawless and incertain thought;" (3.1.128); "stroke and line of his great justice" (4.2.76). It suggests a mind taken up with the complexity—and contradictoriness—of experience: trying to force as much as possible of it into double epithets or verbs with an abrupt change of aspect. And we find a remarkable falling off in the use of this figure in the last two acts.

Something like doubleness of vision or aim is present in words, situations (Claudio's) and characters. And the ethical subtleties we are drawn into half *compel* a casuistic, fine-spinning attention which, despite ourselves, runs beyond the warrant of the text. Even Claudio's "sin" and Angelo's application of the act are double.

Nearly all critics are agreed that there is a break in the play, and that "the last two acts, showing obvious signs of haste, are little more than a drawing out and resolution of the plot" (L. C. Knights). Dr. Leavis calls this view a "casual and confident assumption," and says he finds it "staggering." I find it staggering that he is staggered. It is to me quite evident that the texture of the writing—the tenseness of image and evocative quality—undergoes an abrupt change when the Duke begins talking prose in 3.1.; and that this change applies more or less to all the *serious* matter thereafter. The commentators who are extracting or elaborating themes, of course, do not heed this: though it seems to me a quality that any *literary* critic *must* observe. But Dr. Leavis's terms are evasive, and give the impression that only *theme* is under consideration.

I agree with him that "what one makes of the ending . . . depends on what one makes of the Duke." But I do not quite know what to make of the Duke; and I am confident that it is not the case that he "has been very adequately dealt with by Wilson Knight." Here is Wilson Knight on the Duke: "After rebuking Pompey the bawd very sternly but not unkindly, he concludes: 'Go mend, go mend.'" What is this "not unkindly"?

> Fie, sirrah, a bawd, a wicked bawd!
> The evil that thou causest to be done,
> That is thy means to live. Do thou but think
> What 'tis to cram a maw or clothe a back
> From such a filthy vice; say to thyself
> 'From their abominable and beastly touches
> I drink, I eat, array myself, and live'.
> Canst thou believe thy living is a life,
> So stinkingly depending? Go mend, go mend.

"His attitude," Knight continues, "is that of Jesus to the woman taken in adultery: 'Neither do I condemn thee: go, and sin no more.' (John 8.2)." It is impossible to accept that comment as adequate.

The Jesus-figure of Wilson Knight breaks down in the final scene, where the Duke's treatment of *Lucio* is harsh and not far from spiteful. If you want a *charitable* attitude, read Montaigne, book 3, chapter 5: "*Socrates* to one that told him he was railed upon and ill-spoken of; Tush (said he) There is no such thing in me. . . ." Montaigne comments: "Likewise should any man call me traitour, theefe or drunkard, I would deeme myself but little wronged by him." (*Upon Some Verses of Virgil.*) It is a poor business if a Jesus-figure, or even Dr. Leavis's "Peripatetic Providence," must be sent to Montaigne to learn generosity of mind.

Finally, neither Wilson Knight nor the other interpreters of his group are adequate on the effect of the speech in 3.1 ("Be absolute for death") on the Duke seen as a total character. It is full of Montaigne, but it is not his scepticism: rather the record of its emotional effects on a mind which wants to believe in human magnificence and the nobleness of life—and cannot. It enwraps a death wish far profounder than "Tir'd with all these"; yet is never a cynical dismissal of life as sour grapes, nor a self-dramatizing welcome of death with heroic, histrionic gesture. There is no touch here of "encounter darkness as a bride." It takes away all Man's proud additions, honours, titles, claims—even his selfhood and integrity; and the soul and afterlife are not even dismissed as vain hopes. It cannot be the pseudo-Friar speaking Christian world-contempt: there is no redemption, no hint of immortality in the whole. The only certitudes are existence, uncertainty, disappointment, frustration, old age and death. It mentions values only as delusions. It determines an attitude of mind in which tragedy is quite impossible; in its sombre light all odds [are] gone. Man is a quintessence of dust: Pompey Bum no more nor less than Isabella, nor the Duke above Claudio or Angelo, nor better than Froth, the fool of Mrs. Overdone. Everything exists: nothing has value. We are in the Jacobean equivalent of E. M. Forster's Marabar Caves, of *A Passage to India.*

The Duke absconds from all this by the end of the play: returning as reinstated Justice (which, within this speech, is just another illusion). Meanwhile, Shakespeare has made us feel that there would perhaps be more humanity and kindliness in a world of Pompeys and Lucios, than in one of Isabellas and Dukes of dark corners. We do not know. In the complete and heartaching doubt which is the world of that speech, the world (if it is a world) is one where the accommodated man is the magnificent and horrible *Barnardine.* He lies under sentence of death, and takes life as it comes—in prison ("Denmark's a prison")—content in his filthy straw, usually drunk, "careless, reckless, and fearless, of what's past, present, or to come." His sentence means nothing to him, not even fear of the law. He leaps into greatness with his blunt, unshakeable refusal to be executed to suit anybody's plans: "I swear I will not die today for any man's persuasion." And back to his straw he goes, to sit in state like a judge and condescendingly listen to anything more they have to say.

In this world of tottering values and disordered will, Barnardine stands out as admirable. His will is single: mere will-to-live; and in him the will to be oneself, and to manage others in action by force of mind, reaches a limit. It is one which puts those other characters of action,

Prince Henry, Ulysses, (?) Helena, and even Authority (the Duke) itself, in their right perspectives. I can but suppose he fascinated Shakespeare too; for at the end of the play, in flat defiance of justice and in shocking contrast to Lucio's harsh tit-for-tat treatment, Barnardine is let off scot-free:

> Sirrah, thou art said to have a stubborn soul,
> That apprehends no further than this world,
> And squar'st thy life according.
>
> (5.1.478 ff.)

He is sent off to learn to live—from a Friar. Ridiculous. In the *Measure for Measure* world, he knows already. In the world of these Problem comedies, he is the one positive: man without a mask, entirely assured, unstrippable, "complete." All the rest are doubters and seemers. Develop Barnardine and the Duke's "Be absolute for death," and you pass to Hobbes's picture of the world: where "the nature of man is solitary, fearful, nasty, brutish and short"; a world where force and fraud are the only laws. Yet is not that exactly the world of Iago, that other Sirrah with "a stubborn soul, / That apprehends no further than this world," and squares his life according?

It is only one of the many continuities between the Problem plays and *Othello*: a play about sex, much of it obscene in a nastier sense than most of *Measure for Measure*; a play too of *masks* and crisscross patterns of *seeming* (Desdemona has but little "character," yet there are three of her: ideal, real, and Othello's fantasy of her as a whore). And—as I have remarked of the Problem plays—where love is concerned, there is no standing ground between the ideal and noble, and the base and vile or horrible.

To return to the Duke—and the play's ending. The earlier critics (the Arden editor, for example) are wrong in "character" lines of approach: or if they are not, then the Duke is "consistently inconsistent." Yet if we eschew these lines, and accept the "symbolist/allegorical" interpretation, there is no integrating "Be absolute for death" with the Duke of the end (nor that Duke with the one of earlier acts, such as offering Isabella "revenges"). We cannot get out of the difficulty by saying "He speaks in the role of Friar"; for to omit from Christianity "the resurrection of the body and the life of the world to come" destroys the Christianity: at all events from any seventeenth-century viewpoint—and, I should have thought, from any normal twentieth-century one too.

The *allegorical* reading gives two Dukes at least: the ideal shadow of the end (flawed, for me, by lack of magnanimity) and the realist of a pessimistically contemplated world-order: and in this mixture he is like the whole play, slipping or skidding from the one to the other. The view that he is, like Prospero, an image of Providence, operator of an apparatus for "controlled experiments" to test souls before forgiveness, suffers in the same way. That is why its supporters sidestep the "Be absolute for death" speech, and overlook the lack of charity and forgiveness towards Lucio. To my mind, this interpretation very much depends on two things: (1) on reading Shakespeare's works backwards, beginning with twentieth-century interpretations of the romances, especially *The Tempest* and *The Winter's Tale*; and (2) on this syllogism: God moves in a mysterious way: Duke Vincentio moves in a mysterious way: therefore the Duke is God. There is a piece missing in the syllogism: something missing in the play corresponds to it. Can we, moreover, import into a seventeenth-century play the notions of deity derived from the tormented Christianity of Kierkegaard? If we *can*, then the "Be absolute" lines are a *temptation*—to despair; and Shakespeare ought to have made this clear to us. If what we make of the ending depends on what we make of the Duke, then all I can say is that the Duke (like everybody except Barnardine) is ambiguous: therefore the ending is ambiguous too: and L. C. Knights's essay wins on points.

I believe that *Measure for Measure* was *intended* to finish as a play of a higher ethic, and that ethic "Christian." But this remains largely an aim: achievable by manipulation of the plot (which is why you can take out "the moral fable" and talk about that), but carried out neither by character-development, nor (more important) by the texture of the writing. It goes thin: the earlier tension and realized imagery are absent; and this quality marks a lack of inner conviction. It agrees with the *imposed* quality of the action. There is a solution there: but the "problem" is on one plane, the "solution" on quite another. It is like a wish-fulfillment; or like Ulysses's cosmic order. It ought to apply to existence absolutely: it does *not* apply to experience-as-observed.

> The old "moralities" exemplified most often some rough and ready lesson. Here the very intricacy and subtlety of the moral world itself, the difficulty of seizing the true relations of so complex a material, the difficulty of just judgement, of judgement that shall not be unjust, are the lessons conveyed.

That is Pater on *Measure for Measure.* I find it nearer to the theme of *justice* in Shakespeare's play than most modern interpretations get. It is not perhaps odd that we had to wait for that singularly *Christian* century—our own—to see what Johnson and Coleridge never even noticed? But when I say that, remember that not even an Elizabethan "atheist" could get his mind outside a "Christian tradition."

Last Tuesday—March 4 [1952]—Charles Sherrington died. Who was he? The man who, asking himself what natural religion the twentieth-century man of science can retain, wrote this:

> Its view of the world and of itself is based upon the purview of what by its lights it can accept as true. In that way, for it, much that is comfortable in other religions lapses. If you will, Man's situation is left bleaker. One feature of that situation is that the human mind, such as it is, is left the crown of Mind to which human life in all its needs has direct access. Compared with a situation where the human mind beset with its perplexities had a Higher Mind and Higher Personality than itself to lean on and to seek counsel from, this other situation where it has no appeal and no resort for help beyond itself, has, we may think, an element of enhanced tragedy and pathos. To set against that, it is a situation which transforms the human spirit's task, almost beyond recognition, to one of loftier responsibility. It elevates that spirit to the position of protagonist of a virility and dignity which otherwise the human figure could not possess. It raises the lowliest human being conjointly with the highest, Prometheus-like, to a rank of obligation and pathos which neither Moses in his lawgiving nor Job in all his suffering, could present. We have, because human, an inalienable prerogative of responsibility which we cannot devolve, no, not as once was thought, even upon the stars. We can share it only with each other.
>
> (*Man on His Nature*)

We talk glibly in our literary courses "and their background" of the human situation. We start our "modern age" from the seventeenth century. Why shouldn't it (modernity, *our* human situation) begin with these plays I have ended with today? "We have, because human, an inalienable prerogative. . . ." If you follow what I have been saying, my doubts about "Christian" solutions to *Measure for Measure* will be immediately intelligible.

I can imagine *Measure for Measure* being read, for its humanity, its keen and subtle inquisition into man's nature (into justice and truth, sex and love), by humans in a remote future to whom all the Gospel references belong to a bygone myth—"a local faith called Christianity"—no nearer to them than the gods in Euripides. And I can imagine it holding them none the less, as *we* can be held by the human tangles of the Greek problem-playwright.

Form and Contexts in
Measure for Measure

Herbert Weil, Jr.

Among the most challenging problems presented by *Measure for Measure* is why Shakespeare so thoroughly terminates before midplay the dramatic intensity of his early acts. Although readers and critics have recognized this slackening of tension and suspense, few have been willing to grant that the dramatist may have carefully planned this change of mode. None, so far as I can discover, has shown convincingly why he turns his action to such frustrating anticlimax. Nor has any critic presented a theory of the play's unity that indicates why Shakespeare chose most of the details we find in his last acts. I feel that only if much of the descending action is played in a light comic, often farcical, vein, can all of its speeches fit into a comprehensive design. I use the phrases "light comic" and "broad comedy" to represent passages which aim to arouse our laughter as our *immediate* response. This need not limit the seriousness of the subject matter, the aftereffects, or the implications. Comedy then does not indicate any lack of serious thematic relevance or resonance–unlike the limited seriousness of threats in the fable.

Unless we recognize this increasingly comic mode we cannot understand the unusual formal coherence that Shakespeare creates through his juxtaposition of such discordant elements as potential tragedy and farce. Until the decisive change in act 3, our responses alternate between moderate suspense for the main plot and laughter at the subplot—perhaps mingled with some confusion. After the eaves-

From *The Critical Quarterly* 12, no. 1 (Spring 1970). © 1970 by Herbert Weil, Jr.

dropping Duke Vincentio, disguised as a friar, steps in to interrupt Isabella's angry denunciation of her brother, Claudio, powerful moral and intellectual concerns seem to be ignored. The resulting frustration felt by most readers and critics has been a major cause for two prevalent, but misleading, attitudes toward the final and longer part of the play. One interpretation recognizes that mode and spirit do change drastically in act 3, scene 1, but maintains that thereafter the play is carelessly conceived and carelessly executed. The most common and influential examples of this approach tend to view the play as if it were tragicomic melodrama; they continue to emphasize the threats posed by the villain Angelo. The other approach argues for the play's unity by focussing upon the character of the Duke. But its proponents find this unity only at the expense of neglecting significant speeches which suggest a paradoxical conflict between the Duke's role and his moral attributes. Promptbooks for every production of *Measure for Measure* since 1945 at Stratford-on-Avon show significant cuts in passages that tug against playing the Duke as heroic or as reliable.

Critics seeking excitement and deepening involvement with Isabella or Angelo naturally find the final acts lacking in proper seriousness. Critics who see the play as successfully unified about the Duke, in effect, ask us to believe that the play becomes more serious in its second half—that the seriousness of characters and story are sacrificed for some higher seriousness. In so arguing, they falsify the relaxed confident mood of the final acts. Both of these approaches impose on the play's descending action demands that Shakespeare makes no attempt to satisfy. Consequently they prevent any valid judgment of the unity and accomplishment of the play as a whole. I shall attempt to show how deliberately Shakespeare alters both the mode and structure of his sources and of his own opening acts. With the discordant form that results, he attempts to create an unusual direction for our disappointment at the failure of his action to resolve in convincing depth the moral dilemmas and physical dangers his characters face.

Especially significant is the way in which Shakespeare carefully calls our attention to the extreme shift in subject matter, style, and tone at that moment (3.1.152) when the Duke interrupts Isabella's outburst against her brother. For the remainder of the play, the Duke and the comic characters—Lucio, Pompey, Barnardine—become increasingly prominent. Whenever Lucio or Pompey is onstage, he tends to transform the spirit of the play with irreverent jests. This comic mode, foreshadowed at intervals during the earlier acts, now affects every aspect of the situation of the monstrous proposal—including the Duke who takes it in hand. Those critics who admire him with few reservations lean too heavily on the power of the Duke to avert any catastrophe. They do not explain why he speaks in such an awkward and pompous way nor why he repeatedly makes a fool of himself in response to Lucio and Barnardine.

Because the fifth act of *Measure for Measure* mirrors the structure of the whole play, it supports our discovery of Shakespeare's carefully planned design. As in the complete action, reversal, discordance, and anticlimax are vital. Major moral problems are first convincingly posed and then resolved very superficially or evaded altogether. By treating this final act as a mirror as well as a conclusion, we return to the difficulties created by the use of the spectator's frustrated involvement. Is *Measure for Measure* a better play because Shakespeare engages our minds with significant moral questions—the relation of justice to mercy, of chastity to sexual license—even though the play's action does not work them out in any depth? What finally holds the play together when the author so strikingly changes its spirit and the responses of his audience?

II

Most emphatic among the objections to the descending action of *Measure for Measure* is the preface to the new Cambridge edition by Sir Arthur Quiller-Couch. He accurately observes that, after the Duke intervenes, subject matter and style generally lose the intense vigorous quality of earlier passages. This has been generally accepted, but Quiller-Couch goes on to claim:

> The two halves of this scene cannot be made of a piece by anyone possessing even a rudimentary acquaintance with English prose and poetry . . . We say confidently that the two parts could not have been written by the same man, at one spell, on one inspiration, or with anything like an identical or even continuous poetic purpose.

Although many of us may have shared his disappointment during our first reading, we should not argue from our initial response that there is a major flaw in Shakespeare's design. Shakespeare prepares for this reversal and takes pains to make it so conspicuous. He uses it to signal his audience that they should not feel disturbed suspense over the dangers to the heretofore prominent Claudio and Isabella. The scenes to follow are not melodramatic; they should be played as broad comedy of farcical insults, nonsequiturs, and fantasy.

If the spectator is to feel a radical shift of emphasis after the impassioned debates, the comic elements in the early scenes must not stand out too strongly. But if the shift in tone and emphasis is to surprise the spectator rather than shock or amaze him, the early acts must contain the seeds that make the later change credible. This Shakespeare accomplishes through his use of the comic subplot. In an atmosphere of coarse (and, at times, perhaps intentionally humourless) jesting, we first learn about the central situation of the main plot, the sentencing of Claudio to death. Through Lucio, Pompey, and Mistress Overdone, the spectator further learns about the widespread corruption in the city, about Angelo's proclamations that close the houses of prostitution and reinstate the long dormant death penalty against fornication, and about Isabella at the convent of St. Clare. After feeling offended by Lucio's initial greeting, the heroine quickly recovers and becomes closely linked with him. He accompanies the girl to her first debate with Angelo, and she later defends him against the angry Duke.

In addition to these expository functions, Shakespeare's comic characters help establish an important, unobtrusive rhythm. Repeatedly, an idealistic statement is succeeded by clowning and broad jests. In the first scene of the play, the Duke delegates his power to Angelo, claiming that he has no time to explain his motives, but taking time to expound upon the ruler's duties and the need for mercy. Instead of developing or applying directly any of these principles, Shakespeare shifts to a scene of broad comic gossip and jesting about venereal disease. When we first see Isabella in scene 4, she is requesting "a more strict restraint" upon the sisters of the convent. Lucio then bursts in to interrupt with his mood-shattering, "Hail virgin, if you be." The next scene opens with an argument between Escalus and Angelo, who insists that penalizing fornication with death is proper and that his own virtue will support his extreme decree. But any expectation we might have that Angelo's lines will lead to a straightforward investigation of the nature of justice or to a development of tragic potentialities for the judge or his prisoner is promptly eliminated. The constable Elbow and the tapster Pompey enter, and in the broadest farce of the ascending action use Angelo and Escalus as straight men, constantly interrupting their judges and each other. Angelo reveals mainly his inability to deal with concrete problems of corruption, but he does so in a joyous context that leads to Elbow's defence of his wife:

> If ever I was respected with her, or she with me, let not your worship think me the poor Duke's officer. Prove this, thou wicked Hannibal, or I'll have mine action of battery on thee.
>
> (2.1.814–18)

From this use of comic characters for exposition, atmosphere, and rhythm, we, of course, receive no certain proof that the story will end happily. But such frequent comic interruptions, combined with the audience's knowledge that the Duke is watching over Angelo, should help prevent our feeling that there has been no adequate preparation for the relaxed optimistic mood of the final acts.

Rather than try to hide the disparities between the two halves of his play by involving our emotions, Shakespeare calls our attention to his changes by unmistakable contradictions and discords. As the ascending action of *Measure for Measure* ends in the midst of act 3, scene 1, the highest ethical position of each character in the plot of the monstrous proposal has been shattered. Angelo has learned that his self-controlled purity has been an illusion; Claudio has learned that his resolution to die nobly is weak; and Isabella has shown the audience that her love of mercy is not reflected in her action toward her brother. She cannot sympathize with Claudio's cowardice and his desire to live; her last words to him are:

> Mercy to thee would prove itself a bawd.
> 'Tis best thou diest quickly.

Because these three characters can neither resolve their dilemmas nor face them nobly, it becomes necessary for an outsider to assume control over these problems.

But no sooner does Vincentio step from his hiding place than the play's mode shifts completely into another key. The Duke opens the descending action with praise for Isabella at her most brutal moment, with deceptive lies to Claudio that would deprive him of all hope to live, and with his proposal of the bed-trick. Even the Duke's clumsy prose, full of awkward repetitions, formulas, and clichés, contrasts sharply with Isabella's preceding lines of blank verse ranting. It is surely significant that this transition comes in midscene when we are most likely to notice it.

Such a transition clearly suggests that there will no longer be any real dangers on the story level; it should also prepare us for a dénouement that does not depend on careful moral deliberation. There is little visible need for the Duke's deception of Claudio in such statements as "Angelo had never the purpose to corrupt her [Isabella]" or "tomorrow you must die"; these lies can hardly be accorded the intensity or verisimilitude which the debates have established. Only a few lines later, the Friar introduces his device of the bed-trick which, if it is successful, will contradict his statements to the condemned Claudio. Even if attentive spectators who notice these discrepancies have no ready explanations for them, they would realize that they were no longer to take the dilemmas and dangers of Claudio and Isabella with the seriousness that they deserved in the ascending action. Isabella now need only acquiesce in the devices arranged by the Friar. Claudio does not even receive an honest account of his temporal situation. Until the end of the play, he is rarely on stage and apparently should only prepare himself for death.

The language of the Duke suggests how the mode changes from danger, debate, and moral responsibility to mere justification of non-moral plot devices. He offers a rather long-winded defence of the bed-trick, concluding, "the doubleness of the benefit defends the deceit from reproof." Interestingly enough, Vincentio here, to justify a trick, uses ethical arguments strikingly similar to those Isabella rejected when they were used by Claudio and which her prototype accepted and acted upon in *Promos and Cassandra*. Although she refused to sacrifice her virginity when Claudio, attempting to save his life, begged, "Nature dispenses with the deed so far that it becomes a virtue," she agrees happily to the Duke's scheme for Mariana, "The image of it gives me content already; and I trust it will grow to a most prosperous perfection."

That Shakespeare in *All's Well That Ends Well* and twice in *Measure for Measure* provides extended expository apology for the bed-trick, seems to indicate that he could not, or felt that he could not, rely on the facile acceptance by his audience of this familiar convention. His procedure indicates that he does not want any such unquestioning acceptance; he uses the general mood of his scene and the Duke's clumsy reiterative explanations to Isabella in order to suggest to his audiences that they are no longer watching the same morally serious world as that of the ascending action. This focal scene shows us that he intends us to change our perspective as he changes his tone.

Shakespeare's treatment of the turning point in his action distinguishes him from the writer of melodrama. This term, however anachronistic, describes clearly the dominant mode in the sources and analogues for *Measure*. In effective melodrama, the writer cannot invite a detached and critical response to his plot mechanics, much less burlesque them. The spectator at a melodrama usually suspends any belief he might have that a dire and seemingly inevitable catastrophe will be averted. Because he must not feel any relaxed confidence in a happy ending, he must not be shown how that ending will be reached. In *Measure for Measure,* however, before midplay we share the knowledge of the controlling character and feel sure that the dangers will not come to pass.

Through the remainder of the episodic third and fourth acts, the stage is dominated by the Duke and by comic characters who establish the mood and who insist on commenting about the main action. Shakespeare changes his dramatic focus by repeatedly inventing new, incidental and often comic characters—Mariana, Kate Keepdown, Barnardine, Ragozine, Abhorson—as foils for figures in both main and subplot. These new characters draw our attention from, and tend to decrease our involvement with, Angelo's potential victims, Claudio and Isabella. In addition, Shakespeare reduces the activity of these formerly prominent characters, while he increases that of the Duke. During the descending action either Duke Vincentio or some comic character is present for all but seventy lines. The sequence of substitutions through which Vincentio saves Claudio becomes progressively more farfetched. Although the Duke has successfully preserved Isabella's chastity by substituting Mariana for her in Angelo's bed, his first trick has failed to save Claudio's life. Because Angelo breaks his agreement, Claudio's situation—to outward appearance—remains what it was before either Isabella or the Duke interfered. Conveniently, the Duke discovers a substitute for Claudio, one Barnardine. This prisoner, we learn, is "Drunk many times a day," is "fearless of what's past, present, or to come," and "hath evermore the liberty of the prison; give him leave to escape hence, he would not." Why he is offered the opportunity to run away we never discover, for Barnardine is represented with the minimal credibility he needs to be a foil for Claudio and a test for the Friar. The tone of this episode is set by the first lines spoken to him—Pompey's "Master Barnardine, you must rise and be hanged, Master Barnardine." The condemned criminal refuses the clown, "Away you rogue. I am sleepy." He will treat the disguised Duke in the same way. When the Duke begins his instruction, "Sir, induced by my charity and hearing how hastily you are to depart, I am come to advise you, comfort you and pray with you," the impatient prisoner refuses to listen:

> Friar, not I: I have been drinking hard all night . . . I will not consent to die this day, that's certain . . . I swear I will not die today for any man's persuasion.
>
> (4.3.56–63)

And he does not. After interrupting the Friar-Duke, he storms off the stage, reappearing only in the final act to receive an unconditional pardon.

It is hard to imagine playing this scene as anything other than broad comedy. And it is even more difficult to take seriously the device which finally succeeds in saving the life of Claudio. Only seven lines after Barnardine leaves, the Duke and the audience suddenly learn, "There died this morning of a cruel fever / One Ragozine, a most notorious pirate / A man of Claudio's years." The Duke exclaims, "O, 'tis an accident that heaven provides!" and dispatches his head to Angelo.

Such a fast-paced farcical treatment of Claudio's impending execution eliminates any possible fear or tension the most literal-minded spectator might feel. Even if he has somehow taken quite earnestly the Duke's plans for the substitution of Mariana, the second and third ready-made substitutions would strain his belief. They clearly push too far an initially shaky plot device. Barnardine's unwillingness to serve as a substitute parodies Marian's docility and transforms a grotesque situation into broad comedy. By such exaggeration, Shakespeare signals that he does not wish the spectator to remain emotionally involved with his story.

Barnardine's refusal to cooperate with the Duke climaxes a series of meetings between the disguised ruler and the comic characters. These scenes help to set the tone of the descending action. More important, but less obviously, they reflect essential personal traits in the controlling character himself. For all his power and good intentions, Vincentio, when confronted by a member of the subplot, usually tends to become a comic character himself. The comic aspects of the Duke apparently need stressing because most recent critics who praise the unity of *Measure for Measure* focus on his character or role but tend to omit any thorough discussion of his shortcomings. G. Wilson Knight, F. R. Leavis, Francis Fergusson, and David L. Stevenson treat the Duke either as a symbol for Divine Providence, as a tribute to the newly crowned James I, as the ideal ruler, or as a figure for the author-director, "whose attitude, nothing could be plainer, is meant to be ours." It is often argued that the Duke as director of the action provides its unity by working out some central theme, usually the relation of justice to mercy or of chastity to natural sexual desires. But a unifying theory based upon the virtues of the Duke leaves unexplained such major questions about the final acts as: Why does Lucio so constantly harass the disguised Duke with "compliments" to his lenient rule and his alleged sexual prowess? Why does the Duke-Friar use such clumsy devices to manipulate the action? Why does he tell Isabella in act 5 that her petition for Angelo's pardon is in vain? And why does he repeatedly praise himself with such awkward prose? Studies that discover a neat, allegorical resolution to *Measure for Measure* do not recognize how fully the split in midplay has affected its mode.

Perhaps our best evidence that the reiterated and verbose self-praise by the Duke is not merely awkward or careless writing comes from his direct confrontations with the comic characters. After his interview with Claudio and Isabella, in quick succession Vincentio meets Elbow, Pompey, Lucio and Mistress Overdone. These meetings help create contexts for the Duke's behaviour quite unlike those in the earlier acts when he never confronted any of the comic characters. Now the Duke's reactions to them, usually exaggerated beyond either the requirements of the plot or the demands of verisimilitude, betray his own character. For example, the Duke, just after leaving Isabella, shows his lack of competence and compassion when he sees Elbow and Pompey. Elbow appears only twice in *Measure for Measure*. Each time he is leading Pompey to jail. The parallel responses that the constable and his prisoner elicit, first from Angelo and then from the disguised Duke, provide an important implicit connection between the ruler and his deputy. Vincentio first exclaims, "O heavens! what stuff is here?", and then goes on to berate Pompey:

> A bawd, a wicked bawd!
> The evil that thou causest to be done,
> That is thy means to live. Do thou but think
> What 'tis to cram a maw or clothe a back
> From such a filthy vice . . .
> Canst thou believe thy living is a life,
> So stinkingly depending?
>   (3.2.20–28)

Pompey stumbles, admits that his life does "stink in some sort, sir, but yet, sir, I would prove . . ." The Friar does not permit Pompey to finish. As if forgetting his disguise, Vincentio instructs his constable, "Take him to prison, officer . . . This rude beast will profit." Like Isabella's outburst against Claudio at the climax of the previous scene, the Friar-Duke's attack on Pompey is meant to show us angry vituperation far in excess of any immediate justification. His lines remind us of Angelo's disgust at Elbow and Pompey and his desire that both be punished.

Two choral comments tend to reinforce this exposure of flaws that Vincentio does not recognize in himself. His next speech about "the rude beast" Pompey is a cryptic aside:

> That we were all, as some would seem to be,
> [Free] from our faults, as faults from seeming free.
>
> (3.2.40–41)

With the protracted wordplay and the enforced emphasis of the eighteen monosyllables in this couplet, the Duke shifts the tone of the dialogue and interrupts the action. Vincentio suggests how Pompey (the final "faults") is superior to the idealistic, hypocritical Angelo. The Duke acknowledges—for this one moment—virtues in the comic characters that the spectator has probably long felt. Pompey's essential quality has been captured during his first arrest when he answers Escalus, "I am a poor fellow that would live." When we last see him he gaily presents the most concrete, visual example Shakespeare will provide of reform in corrupt Vienna: "I have been an unlawful bawd time out of hand, but yet I will be content to be a lawful hangman." In this delight, vitality, and flexibility, not in any disgust or morbid cynicism, lies the spirit of the comic subplot. Unlike Angelo, unlike most men, and unlike the Duke himself, Pompey and the comic characters avoid all "seeming" or pretence to a virtue they do not possess.

Lucio, like Barnardine and Pompey, reminds us that Vincentio is not as noble as he thinks himself. Their arguments are central in the descending action, such as Isabella's debate with Angelo had been in the earlier acts. The audience knows that Lucio cannot win, that the Friar is really the Duke. But even with all his advantages, the Duke appears foolish. Often we laugh at the Duke's imperceptive egoism as he turns Lucio's intended compliments into insults. It is clear that Lucio incriminates himself with "pretty tales of the Duke" and of his own wenching.

But if we notice only this obvious, facile self-revelation, we miss completely the richness and suggestiveness of their doubled-edged wit-combats. Lucio first greets the disguised Duke with varied rumours concerning his absence, concluding, "It was a mad fantastical trick of him to steal from the state and usurp the beggary he was never born to." He then leads Vincentio into defending the harsh measures of Angelo. With his most hyperbolic comic metaphors, Lucio declares that, "Angelo was not made by man and woman after this downright way of creation . . . Some report a sea-maid spawned him; some that he was begot between two stock-fishes. But it is certain that when he makes water his urine is congealed ice, that I know to be true." In burlesquing Angelo's view that denies the natural in procreation, Lucio shifts his idiom easily, from fantastic rumour to fantastic certainty. Equally fantastic are the rumours he repeats and his claims to certain knowledge.

Lucio means to compliment the Duke both as ruler and as man by contrasts with the unnaturally cruel Angelo:

> Why, what a ruthless thing is this in him, for the rebellion of a cod-piece to take away the life of a man! Would the Duke that is absent have done this? Ere he would have hanged a man for getting a hundred bastards, he would have paid for the nursing a thousand. He had some feeling of the sport, he knew the service, and that instructed him to mercy.
>
> (3.2.121–28)

Angered by the sexual allusion, Vincentio praises himself, thereby denying Lucio's statements and leading his comic gadfly on to exaggerate, in turn, his alleged knowledge of the "absent" Duke. When the Duke commends himself, "Wise? Why no question but what he was," Lucio now takes the opposite stance, "A very superficial, ignorant, unweighing fellow." Losing all self-control, the angered Duke explodes:

> Either this is envy in you, folly, or mistaking. The very stream of his life and business he hath helmed must, upon a warranted need, give him a better proclamation. Let him be but testimonied in his own bringings-forth, and he shall appear to the envious, a scholar, a statesman, and a soldier.
>
> (3.2.149–55)

I find it difficult to believe that the audience was expected to treat such self-praise as reliable characterization. To interpret the Duke as a tribute to James I, as the ideal Renaissance ruler, or as an allegorical figure for Providence requires that we ignore his angry and wonderfully funny reactions to Lucio.

As Duke Vincentio repeatedly defends Angelo and stresses his own puritanical abhorrence of sex, his resemblance to the deputy becomes much more clear. Although Lucio's allegations may be unfair to the Duke as a private person, they are credible deductions from his negligent practice as a ruler. Ironic self-incrimination is suggested in Lucio's "Friar, thou knowest not the Duke so well as I do. He's a better woodman than thou tak'st him for." Lucio speaks to the character who earlier declared, "Believe not the dribbling dart of love can pierce a complete bosom (1.3.1)." We might well expect such lines from Angelo. The misogyny and pride so emphatically expressed are carefully placed at the opening of scene 3 when the Duke "returns" to Vienna and discloses to the audience the deception he practised in the opening scene. The Duke who moves from this description of himself to propose marriage with the Isabella who wants to be a nun may well be a better "woodman" than he recognizes. Vincentio offers in the lighter contexts of the final half of the play a clear parallel to Angelo's false confidence in his ability to rule efficiently and to resist love or temptation. And Lucio repeatedly scores these failures in the man who "above all other strifes contended especially to know himself."

III

This presentation of the Duke as a well-meaning powerful figure who delights in his own manoeuvring but who fails to understand his own weaknesses will help explain many otherwise perplexing details of act 5. Much of this act must seem trite or irrelevant if one attempts to understand the play either as a romantic melodrama designed to arouse suspense over the fate of threatened characters or as a didactic morality which demonstrates the fair and proper meting out of justice and mercy by the ruler. For example, most commentators have felt that after the Duke reveals that he has saved Claudio, Shakespeare simply forgot to give speeches to the boy and to his sister, for each remains silent. Shakespeare seems, however, to attend carefully in his closing lines to such minor details as the Provost's failure to carry out Angelo's order and the freeing of Barnardine. In fact, Shakespeare in his final lines spends more time on the pardoning of Barnardine and on the punishing of Lucio than on any of the major characters from the monstrous proposal plot.

But Shakespeare's conclusion becomes readily intelligible when we view this last act as a mirror of his structure and strategy throughout the play. In the first part of the scene, we watch the devices of the Duke (about which the audience has been specifically forewarned in the closing moments of act 4) and his comic badgering by Lucio. The Duke's praise for Angelo recalls the play's opening scene; Angelo tries his accusers, Isabella and Mariana, as he judged Pompey. The emotional and ethical climax comes in Isabella's plea that Angelo be spared. Her speech works out a moral pattern that has been implicit since her petition for Claudio. It therefore should not surprise the reader but rather impress him as morally and formally right. Like her suit to Angelo for Claudio, it is refused—to be succeeded, again, by the intentional anticlimax of the Duke's manipulating—his hasty pardons, marriage proposal, and extended dialogue with Lucio.

The need to resolve the main plot, which has hinged on Angelo's "monstrous proposal" and Isabella's response, can explain why the heroine and Mariana accuse the deputy. But only the demands of the broadly comic perspective established by the descending action can account for Vincentio's surprising departure in the midst of the trial when he leaves instructing Angelo as deputy to punish his accusers "to the height of your pleasure."

Why, when Angelo has been truly accused, should be he left to judge his own case? Isabella and Mariana—mingling truth with falsehood—have claimed that Angelo has lain with them. Isabella's false charge has seemed true to Angelo; Mariana's true accusation has made public information about Angelo's behaviour that only the Duke, the two women, and the audience knew. The continued deception is not necessary as a means to trap Angelo. He promptly and simply confesses 100 lines later when Lucio pulls the Friar's hood from the Duke. The multiple lies and Vincentio's unjust delegation of power—which he himself shortly will attack while wearing the Friar's habit—are necessary only so that an aspect of the story, seemingly secondary to the monstrous proposal plot, can be included in the resolution. Shakespeare has constructed his act carefully so that his dramatic emphasis falls upon the disguises and manipulation of the Duke.

When he returns to the stage, again disguised as Friar Lodovick, the Duke, who has always refused to listen to comparable criticism by

Lucio or Pompey, strongly objects to his own policy and rule. Now as he addresses Isabella and Mariana, he claims:

> The Duke's unjust . . . to put your trial in the villain's mouth . . . I have seen corruption boil and bubble till it o'er-run the stew; laws for all faults stand like the forfeits in a barber's shop as much in mock as mark.

These lines have the surface function of leading Lucio on so the Duke can spring his carefully laid trap. But they also bind the Duke's role as ruler more closely to his personal character. Because Vincentio has consistently shown himself to be inefficient and sometimes unmerciful, we cannot consider his initial departure from Vienna and his disguise as mere plot devices.

Only the Duke's desire to emphasize his own tricks and their effectiveness in preserving Claudio explains why the ruler handles Isabella's petition as he does—first carefully shaping the context in which she pleads and then denying her request for mercy. There should be little doubt of the rightness of Isabella's petition. On formal grounds, she makes the only satisfying choice. Isabella earlier told Angelo she would grant mercy if she were in his position; Angelo has repented and confessed; we know his crimes have been only of intent, except for his lying with Mariana, and we certainly expect the final resolution to pardon Claudio for a similar "crime." Perhaps most important, mercy fulfills the highest moral ideal of the play's action. Here in her final speech Isabella shows extremely effective humility and simplicity. Earlier she has shown an idealized devotion to mercy, but no ability to practise it. In her scene with Claudio, we ignore Shakespeare's dynamic moral action if we emphasize the rightness of Isabella's decision to preserve her chastity, rather than the cruelty with which she answers the brother she believes soon to be executed. Because her choice of mercy is not inevitable, her truly merciful behaviour to Angelo is the moral climax of the play. This climax achieves its success largely because it grows from and momentarily transcends the confused and untested values which Isabella upheld. It satisfies us because Shakespeare creates a situation that would permit a cynical or grotesque conclusion—and then rejects the conclusion. He thereby gives us the feeling that, even in this world of Vienna, the morally and logically right decision can be made.

The context in which Isabella pleads is vital. Lucio has just unfrocked the Friar and revealed the Duke; Angelo has been forced to wed

Mariana; the audience and the Duke know that Claudio lives. As the newlywed couple reenter, the Duke, who has just assured Isabella that Claudio is happier because he is dead, now tells her that she must pardon Angelo because he did not achieve his evil intent. But in the same sentence, the Duke continues:

> But as he adjudg'd your brother
> Being criminal, in double violation
> Of sacred chastity and of promise-breach
> Thereon dependent, for your brother's life—
> The very mercy of the law cries out
> Most audible even from his proper tongue,
> 'An Angelo for Claudio, death for death!'
> Haste still pays haste, and leisure answers leisure
> Like doth quit like, and Measure still for Measure.
>
> (5.1.408–16)

Particularly important here is Vincentio's ironic use of the idea of equal substitution and especially of the play's title. Only now, when both the audience and the speaker know that there has been no harm done—that the specific reference to Claudio's death is false—does Shakespeare introduce the title of his play. We cannot accept either the threat of Angelo's execution or the moral appropriateness of the words "Measure still for Measure" in this context because both are contingent upon "An Angelo for Claudio, death for death." The Duke has deprived Isabella's petition of any credible influence on events. Here, as in the pivotal scene where the eavesdropping Friar takes control, moral conflict tends to separate from dramatic action.

That Isabella does not speak again suggests that the dramatist does not want her to detract from the impression she has just created. In his closing lines, Shakespeare deliberately underplays the plot of the monstrous proposal in order to end the action on a comic and anticlimactic note. In one sentence of confused syntax, the Duke, who thoroughly dominates the stage, reveals Claudio, pardons him, and proposes to Isabella:

> If he be like your brother, for his sake
> Is he pardon'd; and for your lovely sake—
> Give me your hand and say you will be mine—
> He is my brother too.
>
> (5.1.495–98)

The wedding of the misogynist Duke-Friar to the chaste novice Isabella, who "most abhors" the sexual vice of her brother, achieves a comic rightness, for Shakespeare combines the formal, conventional resolution with a variation that surprises precisely because neither character has shown the least desire to marry.

The next lines between the Duke and Lucio seem to burlesque not only the hastily presented resolutions in marriage but also the continuing motif of the Duke's fair meting out of justice. Vincentio turns to Lucio with, "And yet here's one place I cannot pardon." As usual, Lucio causes the Duke to betray—in a comic manner—his own weakness as a ruler. The one character who has insulted the manipulating Duke remains his anathema. The Duke demands that Lucio marry the woman he has "wrong'd. The nuptial finished, let him be whipp'd and hang'd." Although Lucio pleads that to marry him to a whore will make him a cuckold, the Duke insists upon the dubious justice of this marriage—which parodies the three other more happy weddings:

> Upon my honour, you shalt marry her.
> Thy *slanders* I forgive; and therewithal
> Remit thy other forfeits.

Lucio's last line, "Marrying a punk, my lord, is pressing to death, whipping, and hanging," may gain him nothing, but once again he reveals Vincentio's ineptitude. The Duke is provoked to contradict explicitly his "forgiveness" of five lines earlier when he replies to Lucio "*Slandering* a prince deserves it."

This concluding scene builds to a dramatic climax which coincides with its moral peak—only to lead to intentionally anticlimactic, nonmoral manipulation. We move from the plot of the monstrous proposal to the bawds with whom the Duke proves so futile. In this comic world, Vincentio has the last word, but he must answer Lucio who has the next-to-last word.

IV

Any criticism of *Measure for Measure* as a unified play must account for rather than evade the implications of its inconsistent details, its fluctuating focus upon different characters, and especially the levels of intensity that distinguish its two halves. For a full understanding of the play, it is necessary to consider the action from two contrasting, overlapping formal perspectives. On one hand, Shakespeare involves us in the situations of his major characters and the dilemmas they face. But he never works these out in convincing depth. This perspective we may call the "problematic" if we use this term as it refers to a work (or major aspect of a work) in which the author poses significant and disturbing moral problems, for which he *intentionally* offers only superficial resolutions. One can readily see that the critic can discuss this perspective only with very limited precision.

On the other hand, when we consider the story in *Measure* and our attitudes toward the threats Angelo poses, we see that Shakespeare offers an increasingly comic approach. The ascending action builds up our concern for Claudio's life and our antipathy toward Angelo because the death penalty seems harsh and excessive. But Shakespeare carefully concentrates his intensity in the first part. The three debates when Isabella faces first Angelo and then Claudio comprise less than 800 lines and all come within the second quarter of the play. Even here, Shakespeare uses Lucio to accompany Isabella when she first meets Angelo and he carefully shows the audience the disguised Duke hiding, but learning all that takes place, when Isabella tells her brother of the deputy's monstrous proposal. The Duke's presence implies the existence of some eternal force that will prevent a direct working out of the dilemmas posed. Once the Duke interrupts Isabella's tirade against her brother, never for more than a moment need we feel concern over the effectiveness of the devices by which Claudio is saved as we would if we were watching an effective melodrama.

In the descending action, the problems of justice, mercy, and sexual promiscuity, posed so forcefully by Isabella and Angelo, remain important, but their relevance often is adapted to the world of Barnardine and Kate Keepdown. The transformation of mood and control proves so complete after the Duke reduces Isabella's dilemmas to such devices as substituting heads or virgins that we must recognize that ethical choices are no longer vital to work out the story. The action of *Measure for Measure* does not lead us to any new discoveries that can resolve bitter conflicts between mercy and justice. In the final scene, as the Duke has contrived the climactic choice, *both* mercy and justice require that Angelo be pardoned. And the final weddings surely are not meant as an earnest solution to the excesses of promiscuity and of chastity—for the last comment on the subject is Lucio's objection that forcing him to marry a punk will make him a cuckold.

Once the critic of *Measure* recognizes its overall comic structure and its increasingly comic perspective, his approach often tends to flatten out or ignore vital distinctions between the early debates and the later farce. Yet the play has become increasingly popular with modern audiences and readers largely because of the early atypical scenes—and their emotional and intellectual engagement which other comedies so rarely can create. While Shakespeare remoulds his overt action, and the moral problems in so far as they are embodied in that action, he expects the alert responsive spectator to feel disturbed. Anticlimactic rhythms and structure call the disparities between problem and solution to the attention of the spectator. Through Lucio and Pompey, the dramatist repeatedly draws our attention to the inadequacy of solutions that the perfectionists in the play—Angelo, Isabella, and the Duke—profess to find adequate. They all share a lack of the self-knowledge which each claims. This false conception leads each to impose demands for extreme purity on those subject to his power, and then to abuse them cruelly when they prove flawed.

Shakespeare, then, creates an action to which we respond in distinct ways. We know that on the level of the fable, no harm will be done. Yet we feel certain that the explanations given by well-meaning, apparently reliable characters do not provide the meaning of the experiences represented. That the Duke saves Isabella and Angelo from the consequences of their self-deception should satisfy us, especially because it comes through their testing and increased awareness. The comic characters, in turn, remind us of the Duke's own pretences and thereby help construct the underlying integrity of the play. The Duke's flaws become laughable because of the contexts in which they are presented and because he does save Claudio and Isabella—as we have long felt confident he would. In this respect, they are similar to the weaknesses of heroes in Shakespeare's romantic comedies. But in keeping with the increased seriousness of tone and subject matter in *Measure for Measure,* they are more consistent and significant. From the perspective of the spectator's immediate response, such flaws suggest a playful comic author. In respect to the thematic issues—the private character of the ruler, the need for mercy and justice, the discrepancies between major flaws and mild effects—all raised in emphatic contexts, we remain aware of unresolved problems as Shakespeare's use of the problematic structure generates a play of mind which is *not* completely reabsorbed by the action itself. It would be a mistake therefore to suggest that *Measure* is completely unified or that any interpretation of it could explain away all disappointment and discomfort. Shakespeare's technique is a daring and experimental one, for this play of mind, held under minimal control, may well become subjective and tangential to the matters actually represented. (The failure of many critics to limit their own play of mind has been one major cause of the general failure to distinguish the internal comic action of the play from its suggestions about the "everyday world" external to the formal action.)

My argument here indicates some ways in which we can discriminate more precisely the mingling of the serious, the comic, and the problematic. Shakespeare again and again calls our attention to the disparity between the emotional involvement with his action and the facile formal resolution that seems inherent in comedy. It is clear that *Measure for Measure* is no attempt at tragedy or melodrama. The excitement of the early acts creates an energy that is not absorbed in the latter part of the play. This energy leaves us appropriately disturbed over the pretences of the characters—pretences perhaps best exemplified by the Duke's misleading praise for Isabella when he interrupts her tirade. But for the spectator, this energy like the suspense, is, for the most part, transformed into a joyous, playful, mocking comedy. Shakespeare parodies the melodramatic structure he took over from his sources. He reveals a hero pompous and apparently successful, yet failing to recognize his own weaknesses. He finally makes us aware of the limitations of the very comic conventions and implausible devices he uses as he stretches them into new possibilities.

Because it combines intellectual vigour and delight with its challenging problematic side, *Measure for Measure* may well be Shakespeare's finest achievement in comedy.

"The Devil's Party:" Virtues and Vices in *Measure for Measure*

Harriet Hawkins

> *Where God hath a temple, the Devil will have a chapel.*
> BURTON, *The Anatomy of Melancholy*

> *Utter my thoughts? Why, say they are vile and false;*
> *As where's that palace whereinto foul things*
> *Sometimes intrude not? Who has that breast so pure*
> *But some uncleanly apprehensions*
> *Keep leets and law-days and in sessions sit*
> *With meditations lawful?*
>
> IAGO

Writing about "the Integrity of *Measure for Measure*" (*Shakespeare Survey Twenty-eight* [1975] Arthur C. Kirsch severely reprimands Dr. Johnson, Coleridge, and numerous modern critics, including myself, for our failure to "take the play's Christian ideas seriously." We are guilty of a "fatal" misunderstanding of the tragicomedy, because we have been either unable or unwilling to place ourselves "in the position of the play's first audience." According to Professor Kirsch, we show an absolutely unforgiving and specifically un-Christian refusal to accept the ending and pardon Angelo, whose libidinousness was miraculously transformed by the bed-trick. Indeed, in the course of his essay, Kirsch goes on to conclude that most of the problems which, over the centuries, have vexed so many commentators, can now be "explained." All difficulties will be made comparatively "easy" by an "apprehension of certain fundamental scriptural texts," and by Kirsch's own scholarly consideration of how

From *Shakespeare Survey* 31 (1978) © 1978 by Cambridge University Press.

those texts "might have been understood and have affected Shakespeare's contemporary audience." Happily, however, this is simply not true. In spite of all Kirsch's arguments, the fact remains that any number of (quite rightly) unanswered questions and unsolved problems seem, whether deliberately or unconsciously, to have been built in to the text of *Measure for Measure* by Shakespeare himself, and these problems and questions are immeasurably more interesting than the solutions to them that have been propounded by modern scholars. For after all, the duty of the artist (as opposed to the scientist) is not to provide us with solutions, but, rather, to make certain that the problems under consideration are accurately posed: "Not a single problem is solved in *Anna Karenina* and in *Eugene Onegin*," wrote Chekhov to his publisher—critic, "but you find these works quite satisfactory . . . because all the questions in them are correctly posed."

Surely no one would deny that serious questions about certain religious values are raised by the action of *Measure for Measure,* as well as its title. But underlying many discussions of its religious references is the facile assumption that the human problems posed here are, theologically at least, soluble, as well as the equally facile (and fallacious) assumption that, back in the good old days of William Shakespeare, there was general agreement about what did, or did not, constitute proper Christian conduct. There was no such agreement. Different people, different denominations, held diametrically opposite views. Confusing "benefactors" with "malefactors" in a series of malapropisms pointed at people like Angelo, poor Elbow reflects a general state of confusion concerning good Christian behaviour:

> I know not well what they are. But precise villains they are,
> that I am sure of, and void of all profanation in the world,
> that good Christians ought to have.

> (2.1.53–55)

Indeed, so far as Christian doctrines are concerned, *Measure for Measure* may itself reflect a kind of dramatic, theological, social, and emotional civil war between dialectically opposed ideologies, and this possibility will get further discussion later on. But first it seems necessary to mention several historical, dramatic, and all-too-human problems in this play that cannot be solved by scholarly appeals to contemporary orthodoxies.

Here are several questions that Shakespeare chose to raise, not to answer, in this particular tragicomedy, and no formalist, thematic, or theological interpretation can answer them for him. How important is physical purity? Given a conflict between Christian virtues, like chastity and charity, which should take precedence? Should, or should not, a brother willingly die for the sake of his sister's chastity? Should, or should not, the sister yield up her chastity to save her brother's life? What if the laws set down in heaven or on earth clash with the biological and psychological laws of human nature? What *about* shotgun weddings (Shakespeare may have had good personal reasons to feel extremely ambivalent about them)? Is not the mutual and free consent of both parties as important in marriage as it is in sex? If it is better to marry than to burn, what constitutes a true marriage? How binding is a legal certificate when there is no marriage of true minds?

And do not the confrontation scenes between Angelo and Isabella establish mysterious and powerful psychological and sexual affinities between them that make incredible the incongruously banal futures assigned them by the Duke? For that matter, what help are pious guidelines from contemporary sermons in those darker realms of human sexuality and psychology so boldly ventured upon, by Shakespeare himself, in this strange course of dramatic events?

Everyone (ask anyone) who knows *Measure for Measure* will surely remember Isabella's searing, shocking, provacative and disturbing refusal to lay down the treasure of her body to the Lord Angelo:

> Were I under the terms of death,
> Th' impression of keen whips I'd wear as rubies,
> And strip myself to death as to a bed
> That longing have been sick for, ere I'd yield
> My body up to shame.
>
> (2.4.100–105)

In its dramatic context, this speech is peculiarly powerful. Everything in it is associated with death, yet Isabella's references to whips and rubies of blood, to stripping herself as to a bed that she had longed for, are charged with an erotic power that might well evoke a gleam in the eye of the most depraved marquis in the audience, to say nothing of a saint-turned-sensualist like Angelo. In its psychological implications, Isabella's speech is like nothing else in Elizabethan drama. Other characters (like Claudio and Antony) associate death with sex; and other threatened heroines of the time (like Whetstone's Cassandra and Jonson's Celia) would prefer torture or death to dishonour. But here and only here—or so a lurid playbill might put it—are fused the red and black extremes of passion and pain, the whips and longings of martyr-dom and desire, of repression and sensuality. Obviously, no commer-cially minded producer would dream of cutting this speech.

Yet perhaps partly *because* of their provocative power, these lines of fire and ice have (so to speak) been given a critical X-rating and effectively banned from many scholarly discussions of the text. If they are cited at all, and they usually are not, they tend to be considered "out of character" or dismissed in a sentence or two: "Isabella ex-presses her readiness to die in erotic terms." Certainly their darker overtones, to say nothing of their obviously sadomasochistic under-tones, are either utterly disregarded or summarily bowdlerized in representative scholarly commentaries like these:

> There is . . . the note of strenuousness, of a kind of moral athleticism which appears in this—as in so many of Isabella's utterances.

> To suppose that Shakespeare gave these burning words to Isabel so that we should perceive her to be selfish and cold is to suppose that he didn't know his job.

> What this speech conveys . . . is that Isabella is afraid not only of Angelo's desires, but of her own.

In effect at least, these dismissive, low-key, reductively easy, or beside-the-point interpretations of Shakespeare's lines would seem ingeniously contrived to defuse a dramatic bombshell that, in spite of all such efforts, will explode in any theatre, in any classroom discussion of the play. They certainly would seem to disregard important evidence concerning the dramatic nature of the confrontations between Angelo and Isabella. So, for the purposes of further argument, here is a discussion emphasizing the perversely fascinating sexual and psycho-logical issues involved.

As Shakespeare reminds us elsewhere, "Lilies that fester smell far worse than weeds." It is, however, when Angelo crosses it that Shake-speare most dramatically erases the fine line between virtuous and vicious forms of human psychology and sexuality that may elevate men (and women) or degrade them. As all the world well knows, Angelo, a man who never feels the "wanton stings" of sensuality, but "doth rebate and blunt his natural edge / With profits of the mind, study and fast" (1.4.60–61) is brought in by the Duke of Vienna to bring back the birch of law. He soon goes beyond all measure in punishing sexual offences, and his self-righteousness immediately begins to manifest itself in sadism: "[I hope] you'll find good cause to whip them all" (2.1.136). *"Punish them unto your height of pleasure,"* says the Duke, much later on (5.1.239, italics mine) when Angelo asks to have his "way" with Isabella and Mariana, thus significantly implying that the bed-trick certainly failed to effect any miraculous transformation so far as Angelo's gratuitous sadism is concerned.

Anyway, from the beginning of the play, the punishment of vice itself turns vicious, misapplied. Furthermore, *virtue* itself enkindles vice when the purity of a young novice ignites Angelo's desire to defile it. "Love in thousand monstrous forms doth oft appear," wrote Spenser, and this is one of them:

> Shall we desire to raze the sanctuary
> And pitch our evils there? O fie, fie fie!
> What doest thou, or what are thou, Angelo?
> Dost thou desire her foully for those things
> That make her good? . . .
> O cunning enemy, that, to catch a saint,
> With saints doth bait thy hook! Most dangerous
> Is that temptation that doth goad us on
> To sin in loving virtue.
>
> (2.2.171–83)

There is a vicious circle here: the saintlier Isabella is, the more Angelo desires her. So perhaps any sincere refusal from her might arouse him still further. Yet her fiery lines, with images of passionate sexuality underlying a prayer for martyrdom, for torture or death, for anything but sexual violation, would seem deliberately designed by Shakespeare to arouse Angelo as saint, as sensualist, and as a sadist. And so, of course, they do. Here is Angelo's response, his answer, his ultimatum to Isabella (for obvious reasons, parallel passages from her speech, which comes less than five minutes before his, are also cited):

	ANGELO: I have begun
	And now I give my sensual race the rein:
Th' impression of *keen* whips I'd wear as rubies,	Fit thy consent to my *sharp* appetite;
And *strip myself* . . . as to a bed	*Lay by* all nicety and prolixious blushes
That longing have been sick for, ere I'd yield	*That banish what they sue for.* Redeem thy brother
My body up	By *yielding up thy body* to my will;

> Or else he must not only die the death,
> But thy unkindness shall his death draw out
> To ling'ring sufferance.
>
> (2.4.158–66, italics mine)

Angelo seems to be recalling, and either deliberately or unconsciously echoing, Isabella's memory-searing lines. She must fit her consent to his "sharp appetite" (his sexual equivalent of "keen whips"?). She must "lay by" (strip herself of) all blushes "That banish what they sue for." In short, she must come to his bed as to a bed "That longing have been sick for" (there is surely a pointed echo in the parallel phrases here). Otherwise, he will have Claudio subjected to prolonged torture before he has him killed. Angelo's lines are far more explicitly sexual, his threats more sadistic, than earlier propositions urging Isabella to ransom her brother with the treasure of her body. They are also far more demanding: he insists upon a completely uninhibited response.

Indeed, one might infer from this ultimatum that Angelo sees in Isabella the feminine counterpart of himself. As he was, so she is; as he is, so she might become. As "black masks / Proclaim an enciel'd beauty," so the saintly asceticism of her life, precisely like his own, may mask a keen appetite that could indeed give full and fit consent to his desire. As he will give the "sensual race the rein," so must she. He will allow her no modesty, no nicety, no blushes to banish what he now believes they sue for. He will have a response equivalent to his own sexual passion.

Reading or hearing these lines, one may well wonder just what might have happened to Isabella in the bed of Angelo. How would she have responded? Could he be right in attributing to her a latent sensuality equal to his own? Who wouldn't like to find that out? Does the fact that Angelo, who was once immune to sex and is now obsessed with it, suggest that Isabella might fall too? Claudio has informed us that

> Liberty,
> As surfeit, is the father of much fast;
> So every scope by the immoderate use
> Turns to restraint.
>
> (1.2.117–20)

So might not the reverse prove true for his sister, as it already has for Angelo? Could her restraint turn to immoderate use? Does her initial desire for more severe restraints within the convent suggest that there is something to restrain? Why does Isabella embrace martyrdom in such passionately sexual terms? Why her special emphasis on woman's frailty? Everyone I've pestered for opinions on her lines says that they seem perfect, exactly in character. I agree, but why so unless the line between saint and sinner, martyr and masochist, righteous severity and sadism—in short, the borderline between angelic and demonic extremes of virtue and of vice—is indeed a very narrow one, and all too easy to cross. At this moment in the play, the psychology, the characterization, and the poetry alike raise all sorts of impious and lurid questions. Who, in an audience listening to inflammatory speeches about stripping and whips, about beds that longing had been sick for, about sharp appetites, sensual races, fit consent, and so on, has a mind so pure but some "uncleanly apprehensions," might "in sessions sit" with meditations lawful?

Far from finding in it affirmations of orthodox pieties, moralists, from Plato to Gosson and Collier, have condemned the drama for inflaming passions and raising impious speculations that they thought ought to be suppressed. Twentieth-century commentators like Kirsch, who tend to presuppose an inveterate piety on the part of Elizabethan audiences, would seem to ignore the obvious fact that there are certain moments in the drama when most members of any audience—Christian or pagan, Elizabethan, modern, or, for that matter, Greek—are virtually forced to join the devil's party, perhaps without knowing it. Given the choice, "you can watch Marlowe's Faustus go forward, or you can watch him repent," how many people would choose the latter? Do we not join forces with Lucifer and Mephistopheles in urging Faustus on towards the midnight hour, to the very heart of darkness? Sometimes, at crucial moments in many works wherein the protagonist has decided to pursue a course of action known by his audience to be dangerous, evil, or inevitably tragic in its consequences, he may be offered an opportunity to desist or turn back. He can then decide (in the words of Macbeth) to "proceed no further in this business." "Ask me no more," pleads Teiresias to Oedipus: "I mean to spare you, and myself," and later on Jocasta implores Oedipus to abandon his tragic quest. Yet who, in the *audience,* wants Oedipus to leave the terrible truth unknown? Shortly before their final encounter with the White Whale, the virtuous Starbuck begs, and momentarily almost persuades, Captain Ahab to return to Nantucket. But does any reader really want Ahab to reverse course? Having come this far, would we not feel, to say the least, let down, if, at this point, Ahab decided to abandon all thoughts of revenge, forget Moby-Dick, and return to his dear wife and children? Similarly, had Faustus heeded the Old Man and managed an eleventh-hour repentance, many members of the audience might well storm out of the theatre demanding refunds from the box office, and complaining, with good cause, about "cop-outs" on the part of Faustus and Marlowe alike.

In certain works, the author arouses a desire, on the part of his audience, for climax, not anticlimax. Thus—sometimes—for the audience, as well as for certain dramatic heroes and heroines, there can be no contentment but in going all the way. Indeed, fictional characters of various kinds may serve as surrogates for our own desire to "try the utmost," to experience whatever it is we most desire, or fear. It is, therefore, satisfying to watch such characters proceed to the outer limits of human experience, and, finally, to watch them face the truths and consequences inherent in our own dreams and nightmares, desires and fears. These facts of dramatic experience seem true regardless of the theological assumptions of the poet's age. So far as *Measure for Measure* is concerned, one may either relish or deplore the psychological and sexual reverberations of Shakespeare's confrontation between a fiery saint and a fallen angel, yet who would not be fascinated by them? Who would not wonder what might have happened, had Isabella yielded herself to Angelo? Where's that palace whereinto "foul things" sometimes intrude not? In the audience? On the stage? Why, incidentally, are Isabella's last lines in the play about Angelo's desire for her?

Given the subsequent course of action, there's no knowing. Shakespeare himself apparently decided, at midpoint in *Measure for Measure,* to proceed no further in this business—or, as Dryden would put it, having first prescribed a purge, he immediately orders us to take restringents. There is, clearly, a deliberate and virtually complete withdrawal from this (his and our) fascination with the sexual and psychological proclivities of his villain and his heroine. Perhaps significantly, he never again permits them a moment alone together on the stage. He abruptly and conspicuously parts company with his sources, wherein the counterpart to Isabella *always* yields up her body, for one night, to Angelo's counterpart. But, then, in none of his sources is the sexual and emotional situation anything like so highly charged. Perhaps partly to avert a conflagration, Shakespeare resorts to a series of elaborate intrigues. He drags in the tepid Mariana to play the bed-trick, thus assuring that Angelo is securely fettered to another woman by the bonds of holy wedlock, and then—ever widening the safety zone between his incendiary pair—he has the Duke claim Isabella for his own. Thus, officially at least, Shakespeare precludes further speculation about a sexual moment-of-truth between Isabella and Angelo. In short, the subsequent action of the play, like many scholarly discussions of it, would seem designed to encourage us to efface from the memory the extraordinary psychological and sexual reverberations of the earlier scenes. Assuming (only assuming) that Shakespeare himself wants us to disregard that dramatic evidence which he himself introduced previously, is it, in the last analysis, possible to do so?

Obviously, a master-poet like Shakespeare may consciously, or unconsciously, incite powerful emotional responses from us in any number of different ways. But it is sometimes impossible for even the greatest writer to suppress strong emotional responses which he has already, either in intent or in effect, aroused in his audience. Shakespeare's leading expert on the permanent effect of provocative sexual imagery is, of course, his very own devil-in-the-flesh, Iago. Precisely like an unethical counsel-for-the-prosecution of Desdemona, Iago intrudes all sorts of inflammatory images into Othello's mind, and then tells Othello to take no further notice of them:

> I do beseech you—
>
> . . . .
> that your wisdom yet,
> From one that so imperfectly conceits,
> Would take no notice, nor build yourself a trouble
> Out of his scattering and unsure observance.
>
> (3.3.148–55)
>
> My lord, I would I might entreat your honour
> To scan this thing no further;
>
> . . . .
> Let me be thought too busy in my fears—
> As worthy cause I have to fear I am—
> And hold her free, I do beseech your honour.
>
> (3.3.244–48)

Thus, in legal terms, Iago "objects" to his own testimony, and instructs Othello to "disregard the evidence." Or, in common parlance, he advises Othello to lock the barn doors of his imagination after having already loosed the wild horses. As his own rhetoric implies (he deliberately protests too much), Iago knows the answer to that age-old courtroom question: "How can a jury disregard evidence already presented to it?" The answer is, "It can't." Potent evidence may finally be outweighed by equally potent evidence, emotions can be countered by equally powerful emotions, but no one can, by taking thought, obliterate from the imagination associations implanted in it by the very command to do so: "Try to count to ten without thinking of a rabbit." Thus, even as he urges him to put them out of mind, Iago effectively sears his "dangerous conceits" into Othello's imagination and memory:

> Dangerous conceits are in their natures poisons,
> Which at the first are scarce found to distaste,
> But with a little act upon the blood,
> Burn like the mines of sulphur. I did say so.
>
> (3.3.325–28)

Iago spoke these lines before a court audience on November 1, 1604. It goes without saying that the creator of Iago knew—none so well as he—all about the survival power of sexually and emotionally charged "conceits." And he certainly knew it when Isabella first spoke her inflammatory lines to Angelo at the court of King James on December 26, 1604. Had he wished to, surely he could have—and would have— toned down those confrontation scenes.

Yet he didn't. Why not? He certainly had reason to, if he wished to provide us with easy solutions to the problems posed. For that matter, why doesn't Angelo say that his lust for Isabella represented a perverted appetite, and that he has finally realized his true love for Mariana? Why doesn't Isabella say that she has learned what it means to be a woman from Mariana and therefore accepts the Duke's proposal of marriage? Why did Shakespeare leave it to scholars, centuries later, to provide these solutions for him.? Surely an obvious problem with the text as it stands is that the subsequent intrigues do not serve to set what has gone before in a new light, nor to overwhelm us (as Emilia overwhelmed Othello) with a new blaze of truth, but perfunctorily and ineffectually to contradict the earlier characterization and action and so, perhaps, confuse and frustrate us. Coleridge, for one, found the ending too good to be true. Seeing in this play something "horrible," seeing sadism and criminal sexuality in him, it was impossible for Coleridge to accept "the pardon and marriage of Angelo": "For cruelty, with lust and damnable baseness, cannot be forgiven, because we cannot conceive of them as being morally repented of." Whatever

Shakespeare might wish him to do at the end of a play ostensibly concerned with forgiveness, Coleridge (who, like Dr Johnson, was a devout Christian as well as a great critic) cannot do this: cannot forgive, cannot conceive, cannot imagine. Neither could most commentators until the twentieth century.

In recent years, Shakespeare's scholarly jury has been hopelessly split between those who can, and those who cannot, those who will, and those who will not, accept the ending of *Measure for Measure*. Those who cannot (like Coleridge) tend to be concerned with the major characters, with the consistency (or inconsistency) of their psychology, their motives, and their behaviour, and with the powerful emotional responses which they elicit. Critics who approve of the ending (like Kirsch) tend to be primarily concerned with the play's tragicomic form, its themes, and its religious overtones.

This critical deadlock surely results from problems inherent in the text itself. For though he clearly sets out to explore them, here, as elsewhere, Shakespeare was not about to subordinate his apprehension of a most protean reality to any single doctrine, dogma, or dramatic form. Throughout *Measure for Measure* there is a kind of firelight flamenco dance between comedy and tragedy, piety and impiety, virtue and vice, wherein one may threaten, arouse, change places with, embrace, or repulse, the other. So far as sexual vices and virtues are concerned, Shakespeare would seem to have here developed the photonegative reversals, the strange changes and interchanges between benefactors and malefactors that he describes in *Romeo and Juliet*:

> For nought so vile that on the earth doth live
> But to the earth some special good doth give,
> Nor ought so good, but strain'd from that fair use,
> Revolts from true birth, stumbling on abuse.
> Virtue itself turns vice, being misapplied;
> And vice [sometime's] by action dignified.
>
> (2.3.17–22)

The sexual act between Claudio and Julietta, the one most severely condemned throughout the play, is, paradoxically, the only one in it that is dignified by mutual love. What is commonly deemed the "vilest" form of sex, commercial prostitution, with all the diseases it entails, seems comparatively harmless when set beside Angelo's "sharp appetite" and "salt imagination," that is, when set beside the diseases of the soul.

Sometimes to avoid "all profanation in the world" is to invite disaster. As J. C. Maxwell put it, it is certainly possible, "without manifest distortion," to see the germs of twentieth-century psychological ideas in this play: "I have even been told of untutored playgoers who thought that it was Jonathan Miller and not Shakespeare who conceived the notion of setting it in Vienna." For that matter, the fact that sexual repression could result in neurosis, in a diseased imagination, in sexual aberrations, was as obvious to Freud's Elizabethan predecessor, Robert Burton, as it was to Shakespeare.

In *The Anatomy of Melancholy*, Burton (very like Shakespeare in *Measure for Measure*) brings together "Great precisians" and "fiery-spirited zealots" as well as certain types that (by the way) surely composed a substantial part of Shakespeare's audience: there are the "good, bad, indifferent, true, false, zealous, ambidexters, neutralists, lukewarm, libertines, atheists, etc." In Burton, as in Shakespeare, virtue itself may turn to vice: "Howsoever they may seem to be discreet," the "preposterous zeal" of great precisians (like Angelo) can result in forms of madness that may break out "beyond all measure" (3.372). In sexual matters, by seeking to avoid Scylla, one may fall into Charybdis, and "Venus omitted" may do as much damage to the body and mind as "Intemperate Venus": it may cause "priapismus, satyriasis, etc." and "send up poisonous vapours to the brain and heart." If the "natural seed be over-long kept (in some parties) it turns to poison" (1.234). For that matter, the tyranny of religious "superstition" seemed as terrible as the tyranny of princes: "What power of prince or penal law, be it never so strict," asks Burton, could enforce men, and women like Isabella, to do that which they will voluntarily undergo, "As to fast from all flesh, abstain from marriage, whip themselves . . . abandon the world?" (3.332). Zealots of this kind will endure any misery, "suffer and do that which the sunbeams will not endure to see, *religionis acti furiis*," endure "all extremeties," "vow chastity," "take any pains," "die a thousand deaths" (3.350).

Might not organized religion itself, rather like the Duke—or like oversimplified, "Christian" interpretations of *Measure for Measure*—provide solutions that are false, ways out that are too easy? Discussing, and deploring, the "general pardons" issued by Catholics (their "easy rates and dispensations for all offences") Burton observes how "their ghostly fathers" so "easily apply remedies . . . cunningly string and unstring, wind and unwind their devotions, play upon their consciences with plausible speeches and terrible threats, . . . settle and remove, erect with such facility and deject, let in and out" (3.403–4). I have never seen, anywhere, a better gloss on the dubious contrivances of Shakespeare's Duke-disguised-as-a-friar than this. Even in the end, when the organization of the play seems to encourage it, the characterization seems to subvert an acceptance of the Duke's far too facile settlements and solutions: Angelo asks only for death, never for marriage to Mariana; Isabella's response to the Duke's proposal is silence. In the end, as in the beginning, they seem, oddly, two of a kind.

Moreover, by way of their counterparts on the stage (Claudio, Lucio, Barnardine) this play might seem quite sympathetic to the ordinary sinners in Shakespeare's audience. Markedly unlike the Duke, Shakespeare's play does not "repel a fornicator, reject a drunkard, resist a proud fellow, turn away an idolator, but entertains all, communicates itself to all." It is in this spacious humanity, and, perhaps, only in this, that Shakespeare might be said to reflect the ultimate grace of God. Yet he also gives the devil his due. In the confrontation scenes, as Coleridge observed, he confronts us with things that are "horrible." He crosses the boundary between the angelic and the demonic to remind us that God's temple itself may contain the devil's chapel. Through his recalcitrant characters, he challenges the assumption that human nature can be made to perform according to a scenario of the Duke's contriving. Critical efforts to exorcize the play's demons, to disregard Shakespeare's illumination of the darker regions of the soul, in effect deny the play one of its boldest claims to truth. And to impose any external—thematic, formalist, or theological—solutions on the manifold and enduring problems posed within it is, in fact, to deny this play its rightful claim to greatness. Finally, it seems impertinent to consider it the duty of criticism to solve problems that Shakespeare himself refused to solve. What remain pertinent are the problems posed.

Providential Improvisation in *Measure for Measure*

Louise Schleiner

Measure for Measure seems to have a chameleon quality, so radically can its complexion change. After the nineteenth-century aversion to the play and its characters had given way to the Christian rehabilitation by Wilson Knight, R. W. Chambers, Roy Battenhouse, and such discriminating qualifiers as Elizabeth Pope and Nevill Coghill, a return of the pendulum brought us back to the dark, satiric *Measure* of Clifford Leech and A. P. Rossiter, whose still-productive strain of criticism says that the Duke, far from being God, is an unpleasant busybody who flees responsibility in a world of salacious seediness that he can cope with only through incredible tricks. Consistent with this view is the idea that Shakespeare was "disillusioned with the art of comedy" and here stretched comic form past the breaking point. Perhaps these tendencies have reached their apogee in such productions as that of a recent Ashland Shakespeare Festival, where the opening curtain revealed the Duke rapt in sadistic fantasies of hanging, twisting nuns, then pronouncing his lines about the nature of government in frenzied distraction and fleeing his ducal rule for fear of his own sexuality. Is this the black-robed, red-crossed, fatherly figure we used to see? No other Shakespeare play has left us in doubt whether the hero is God or a poor man on the verge of nervous collapse.

No one well acquainted with both the New Testament and Shakespeare's plays can believe that the "Christian coloring" of *Measure for Measure* is merely incidental. In no other play do the central characters

From *PMLA* 97, no. 2 (March 1982). © 1982 by the Modern Language Association of America.

evoke specific biblical passages and theological concepts to explain their crucial deeds; in no other are the allusions so prominent; in no other do they define so distinct and consistent a pattern. The Duke need not be God, but we must account for these allusions somehow: this is Shakespeare's most theological play. Lucio's "old fantastical Duke of dark corners" (4.3.157) must be exposed, not so much in his sexual as in his theological (and theologically political) nature.

The present essay argues that the many New Testament references evoke an ironically employed theological pattern framing the play's central action; that although the Duke attempts to imitate God he is not God but a ruler dissatisfied with his past government whose efforts to imitate God in justice and mercy (as rulers were theoretically supposed to do) produce comic results; that he is a man of tests, a character modeled on the absentee-master figure in a group of parables from the synoptic gospels; that his test results prove so discouraging that they force him to imitate another aspect of the New Testament God as well, the legal astuteness of the Pauline God, who in the atonement "found out a remedy," a kind of divine lawyer's trick, for guilty man; that the play's falling in half as discussed by Tillyard results from this planned and necessary expansion of the Duke's strategy; that his schemes, though imperfect and comical improvisations, aim to bring the characters to their best selves and do not degrade the Duke to a mere meddler; and finally that there is a strong earthiness in the play, a forceful dramatization of the power of the drives for food, drink, sex, and comfort—drives that throughout the play challenge the authority of the Duke and his deputies. This strain reaches a climax in Barnardine's sleepy growl from the depths of the prison and his subsequent comic line, "I swear I will not die to-day for any man's persuasion" (4.3.59–60).

The Duke's decision to delegate his rule and disappear—and this derivation has received hardly any notice—the Duke's decision has as its primary model the parables of the synoptic gospels that state or imply that a man planning a journey or absence called in servants and gave them responsibilities. These are the parables of the wicked vineyard tenants (e.g., Matt. 21:33–43); the wicked steward (e.g., Matt. 24:45–51); the traveler and his doorkeeper (Mark 13:33–37); the master absent at a wedding (Luke 12:35–39); and the talents or pounds (e.g., Luke 19:11–27). A departing ruler or land owner gives responsibility to servants, who will be called to an accounting on his return, for which they are to be constantly ready. The master's destination or motives abroad are of no importance; the servants are to be tested and later rewarded. In his commission to Angelo, after his gospel analogy "Heaven doth with us as we with torches do, / Not light them for themselves" (Matt. 5:14–16), the Duke alludes to the talents or pounds parable:

> nor Nature never lends
> The smallest scruple of her excellence,
> But like a thrifty goddess, she determines
> Herself the glory of a creditor,
> Both thanks and use.
>
> (1.1.38–42)

The testing master, lending different amounts to the servants according to each one's capacity and expecting a corresponding return with interest, is here figured as the goddess Natura, pehaps on the assumption that the testing aspect of God is simply part of the nature of creation. But "the glory of the creditor" is a strange phrase, given the reputation of usurers at the time. The Duke seems unintentionally to cast an ironical light on his deed. At any rate, he thus aligns himself with the testing master, Angelo and Escalus with the commissioned servants.

In his relationship with every other character the Duke retains this stance. Critics have sometimes read his testing urge as heartless scientific curiosity, a view that does not accord with his constant concern for his subjects' well-being. Some have found him a deeply mysterious figure, but his character appears at least conceptually consistent once we recognize this moral testing as its mainspring. Commitment to searching out and supporting the right and the good is his leading trait, as the gossip's flippancy is Lucio's, lofty idealism Isabella's. We can partly explain the aversion of many modern audiences to his bed trick and other manipulations by considering that we no longer accept moral correction from civic authorities or even from clergy—only from psychiatrists and other doctors. (The psychiatrist in T. S. Eliot's *The Cocktail Party* resembles our Duke.)

Many critics have analyzed the Duke's testing of Angelo and Isabella, but we should notice that the Duke also tests the minor characters by observing their conduct from his absentee perspective and then determining appropriate judgments. He alludes again to the parable of the talents in his final words to the provost. Earlier he has said, "This is a gentle Provost: seldom when / The steeled jailer is the friend of men" and "There is written in your brow, Provost, honesty and constancy; if I read it not truly, my ancient skill beguiles me" (4.2.86–87, 153–55). Now in the final lines of the play he says, "Thanks, Provost, for thy care and secrecy, / We shall employ thee in a worthier place" (5.1.530–31). As the good servants heard, "It is wel done good servant and faithful, Thou hast been faithful in litle, I will make thee ruler ouer much" (Matt. 25:21). In the Lucan version of the parable the servants include some who have not merely proved "unprofitable" but have actually spoken against their lord: "Moreouer those mine enemies, which wolde not that I shulde reigne ouer them, bring hither, and slay them before me" (Luke 19:27). This version may have provided a model for the Duke's harsh judgment of Lucio, a death sentence remanded to the comically appropriate marriage to the whore Lucio has slandered in the same breath with the Duke.

Most of the other absentee-master parables also are echoed in *Measure for Measure*. As Wilson Knight notes, Angelo is a wicked steward who, thinking himself safe, begins "to smite the servants and maidens." "The master of that servant wil come in a day when he thinketh not; and at an houre when he is not ware of, and wil cut him of, and giue him his portion with the vnbelievers" (Luke 12:46). As the Duke in disguise puts it, "within these two days he [the Duke] will be here. This is a thing that Angelo knows not; for he this very day receives letters of strange tenor . . ." (4.2.199–201); and in the next scene, "By cold gradation and weal-balanc'd form, / We shall proceed with Angelo" (4.3.100–101). Or is the master away at a wedding, his servants required to watch and wake for him (Luke 12:35–39)? The Duke is busy about four weddings. Does the master return suddenly from a journey and test his doorkeeper (Mark 13:33–37)? Shakespeare has the Duke order Angelo and Escalus to stand at the city gate to return his authority, as if they were door wardens.

Measure for Measure is not itself a parable, but these New Testament parables, the most famous of which is alluded to at the beginning and again at the end of the play, provided a model for the Duke's character from start to finish. Thus Shakespeare set up from the beginning our expectation that the Duke would "return" and pronounce judgments—though as befits a comedy mercy prevails and his harshest sentence is sexual "death" in marriage. Tillyard does not take this pattern into account in his influential discussion of the play. He argues that the play divides in half because the Duke does not begin his machinations until the second part, while the first part presents realistic, self-actuating characters and keeps the Duke in the background. That the play changes tone in the middle, as Tillyard shows stylistically, is true enough, but the Duke, though perhaps not totally consistent, is the testing master from beginning to end. As he says in act 1, scene 3, he contrives the opening situation to test Angelo, Escalus, and the government he expects of them. Act 2 reveals him busy testing Juliet's penance and Claudio's readiness for death. In act 3 he evaluates Pompey, tells him "Go mend, go mend," and declares that Pompey should be imprisoned. Certainly the Duke appears often enough to keep his controlling experiment in our minds. The reason he does not intervene more actively at first is that he intends his testing to be detached, a matter of observation and analysis: "And to behold his sway, / I will, as 'twere a brother of your order, / Visit both prince and people" (1.3.43–45). He even shows himself willing to allow Claudio's execution, as long as Angelo's rectitude makes it just by the principle of the title passage, "with what measure ye mete, it shall be measured to you again" (Matt. 7:2). Only when Angelo's injustice is revealed does the Duke intervene, and his tactics simply continue his testing: he now sets up new tests, just as he had set up the first one and followed up its results.

If the Duke is modeled on the absentee testing master of the parables, why is he not really absent? Whetstone's king, in Shakespeare's source, commissions the deputy from elsewhere and arrives only late in the play. But the Duke's presence in disguise does not obviate the role of testing master—a seeming absence suffices. Of course the divine Master of the biblical parables is never really absent either—only seemingly so. Shakespeare adopted a radically new conception of the story, importing the bed trick to thwart Angelo's evil deed. He wanted each major character rescued from the most destructive impulses of his or her own nature. Angelo need not go under in the first gush of his long-repressed sexuality. Isabella, whose verve, idealism, and rhetorical ability differentiate her sharply from the source character, need not be raped; her naive spiritual pride could be broken less brutally. Claudio need neither die nor consent to his sister's rape— surely in some more appropriate way he could be made to recognize the petty greed and falseness of holding out for a bigger dowry while secretly enjoying Juliet as his wife. With the importation of the bed trick and the faithful Mariana, the Duke becomes a necessary overseer. Thus the simple king of the earlier story becomes the unseen testing master, attempting to watch providentially.

The Duke must be present and his role must expand midway in the action, since he must first test and observe, then devise a remedy for the failures, as a teacher seeing the whole class has flunked a test must devise a new pedagogical strategy and new tests. As a counterpoise to Angelo's declaration concluding act 2 ("now I give my sensual race the rein") comes the Duke's "craft against vice" speech concluding act 3, making quite clear to the audience why he has begun to intervene; the rhymed tetrameters lift this speech out of the play's blank verse to give it the needed air of major pronouncement. Shakespeare is sometimes pictured as having written himself dry in acts 1 and 2 then having improvised wildly to resolve his difficulties. But it is the Duke who improvises wildly. Given the theological pattern I will describe more closely, given the controlling concept of the Duke's role as comical *imitatio dei,* it appears that Shakespeare planned the shift all along.

For the Duke to work the bed trick convincingly, he has to be shocked out of his objectivity, to be convinced that only the most radical measures will serve. The exchange he overhears between Claudio and Isabella—the news of Angelo's treachery, Claudio's loss of nerve, Isabella's hysteria—does just that. At that point he could of course simply "return" and depose Angelo, but the keen eye of the testing master sees a way to get a far better profit on his moral capital. If the Duke should reappear, Angelo would simply deny everything and remain locked in his hypocrisy. Isabella would go back to the convent, her pride and prudery vindicated. Claudio, in righteous indignation, would forget how his own petty greed had led him into this trap, and furthermore he might, as Angelo fears, attempt retribution. Juliet's heartfelt repentance would appear misguided.

No, the Duke sees a better way: "to the love I have in doing good a remedy presents itself" (3.1.198–99). Coming from the testing master, the word "remedy" may remind us of Isabella's words to Angelo in the previous act:

> Why, all the souls that were were forfeit once,
> And He that might the vantage best have took
> Found out the remedy
>
> . . . .
>
> O, think on that,
> And mercy then will breathe within your lips,
> Like man new made.
>
> (2.2.73–79; cf. many Pauline passages)

The Duke now recognizes that, while remaining a tester, he must try to imitate God on another level as well. He must find a remedy to bring new life to his subjects.

> Craft against vice I must apply.
> With Angelo to-night shall lie
> His old betrothed (but despised);
> So disguise shall, by th' disguised,
> Pay with falsehood false exacting,
> And perform an old contracting.
>
> (3.2.277–82)

The loving Mariana is to substitute for Angelo's victim and bear the brunt of "death" as Christ bore it for mankind. Again the Duke, by imitating God, seems to cast both God's ways and his own in a comical light, from the perspective of the law: perhaps the atonement too was "craft against vice," God in disguise as man paying the devil's false exacting, a divine trick to get off the guilty defendant. The theological overtones cannot be accidental, cast as they are in the play's pattern of biblical allusions. But how are they to be taken—sententiously, ironically, or perhaps as part of a pattern that is ironically employed, but sometimes light-heartedly, sometimes darkly?

Further review of the theological allusions clarifies the question. After the Duke invokes the "talents" in 1.1 to explain his abdication, in 1.2 Lucio (jokingly) and Claudio (in bitter earnest) introduce the theme of salvation by grace (foreshadowing the later phase of the Duke's role). As Lucio and his rakish friends trade witticisms on whether all ten commandments must be kept or whether some may be "razed" and on which sectarian form of "grace" should be said before meals, Lucio declares: "Grace is grace, despite of all controversy; as for example, thou thyself art a wicked villain, despite of all grace" (1.2.24–26). The exchange parodies sectarian emphasis on salvation by grace to the exclusion of good works. Then Claudio comes on with his comment about the shame and death Angelo is inflicting on him.

> Thus can the demigod, Authority,
> Make us pay down for our offense by weight
> The words of heaven: on whom it will, it will;
> On whom it will not, so; yet still 'tis just.
>
> (1.2.120–23)

Claudio is summarizing Rom. 9:11–27 to declare that Angelo's arbitrariness in singling him out for condemnation is like the arbitrariness of God in choosing whom to save, whom to damn.

Since these lines are often misread to mean that Claudio accepts his sentence as "just," we must look at the passage referred to.

> As it is written, I haue loued Iacob, & haue hated Esau. What shal we say then? Is there vnrighteousnes with God? God forbid. For he saith to Moses, I wil haue mercie on him, to whome I wil shewe mercie: and wil haue compassion on him, on whome I wil haue compassion. So then it *is* not in him that willeth, nor in him that runneth, but in God that sheweth mercie. For the Scripture saith vnto Pharao, For this same purpose haue I stirred thee vp, that I might shewe my power in thee, and that my Name might be declared through out all the earth. Therefore he hathe mercie on whome he wil, & whome he wil, he hardeneth. Thou wilt say then vnto me, Why doeth he yet complaine? for who hathe resisted his wil? But, o man, who art thou which pleadest against God? shal the thing formed say to him that formed it, Why hast thou made me thus? Hathe not the potter power of the Claie to make the same lompe one vessel to honour, and another vnto dishonour? *What* and if God wolde, to shewe his wrath, and to make his power knowen, suffre with long pacience the vessels of wrath, prepared to destruction? And that he might declare the riches of his glorie vpon the vessels of mercie, which he hathe prepared vnto glorie?
>
> (Rom. 9:13–23)

"Yet still 'tis just" is not Claudio's evaluation of his sentence but the conclusion of his summary. "On whom it will, it will; / On whom it will not, so; yet still 'tis just." Thus succinctly he sums up this notorious predestinarian passage. Though Claudio, in the famous surfeit-and-fast speech, recognizes that he has violated the golden mean, has failed to moderate his love for Juliet, he by no means accepts the justice of public disgrace and death as punishment. He reasons that Angelo is making an example of him, that the sentence is "tyranny" (1.2.163), and that Angelo's motive is to show off his power: "for a name / [he] Now puts the drowsy and neglected act / Freshly on me—'tis surely for a name" (1.2.169–71). This logic corresponds precisely with Paul's only explanation, in the passage from Romans, of God's elections: to the pharaoh who has suffered the plagues God explains that it was "that I might shewe my power in thee, and that my Name might be declared through out all the earth." (We may note too that the Duke, exactly as God is said to do, will "suffre with long pacience the vessels of wrath," i.e., will refrain for a time from punishing the sinners he sees, in order to carry out his plans for redeeming the major characters.)

In terms of religious politics Lucio's and Claudio's allusions glance at Angelo as a Puritan. In terms of the play's image of the ruler as *imitatio dei,* the repercussions go further and become ominous. If the Duke in imitating God attains the "glory" of usury, his deputy in trying to do the same attains the "tyranny" of arbitrary condemnation. This scene makes us wonder whether God's ways can possibly serve as a model for rulers. Grace may be grace despite of all controversy, but why do some receive it and others not? How can civil law be based on any such concept? Pompey, Lucio, and the like will remain as they are, "despite of all grace" yet without earthly punishment, while Claudio, for a far lesser offense, is to lose his head. Claudio here shakes his fist at the predestinarian's "heaven" as well as at Angelo. The dark and bitter mood so many critics have sensed in acts 1 and 2 is indeed present, and this challenging of supposed heavenly as well as earthly justice is part of it. As Escalus says, musing on Claudio's case,

> Well, heaven forgive him! and forgive us all!
> Some rise by sin, and some by virtue fall;
> Some run from brakes of ice and answer none,
> And some condemned for a fault alone.
>
> (2.1.37–40)

Like several other questioning moments, this one is followed by a cynically humorous scene that acts out its point: Elbow drags Pompey and Froth to a hearing but proves incapable of formulating his charge, so that they escape totally unpunished, though Escalus obviously perceives their guilt. The humor in *Measure for Measure* is very funny, but it is a kind of black humor, reinforcing the themes of hollow justice and tyrannous authority. Josephine Bennett's effort to declare Claudio's death sentence a mere fairytale device and thus to explain away the seriousness of acts 1 and 2 has not won wide acceptance. As R. G. Hunter demonstrates, the death penalty for fornication as well as for adultery was advocated by Elizabethan Puritans and eventually enacted under the commonwealth. Angelo is Shakespeare's projection of the possibility of this enactment, and the fears of acts 1–3 cannot be lightly dismissed.

Fast upon this scene with Elbow, Pompey, and Froth follow Angelo's interviews with Isabella and his wicked proposition. The Duke says he is going to apply craft against all this vice, and surely, we think, things will start being set to rights. Donning the mantle of God redeemer over the traveling cloak of God the absentee tester, the Duke finds Isabella acquiescent to his scheme, but his nerve fails when it comes to putting the proposition to Mariana. Though he has promised Isabella he will "frame" the maid and make her "fit for his attempt" (3.1.256), he hems and haws and leaves Isabella to propose the scheme to her. The redemptive substitution here suffers a radical diminution. If the Duke playing God the tester seems a moral usurer, if Angelo playing God the judge sounds tyrannous (even before his lust), the Duke and Isabella soliciting Mariana to play Christ the substitute victim give off a whiff of procurement. Scene 2, immediately following, brings on Pompey the bawd punning on his "stinking" profession.

Having seen this much of the play's ironic underside, however, we must recognize that Shakespeare goes out of his way to show Mariana as a lady of depth and honor, certainly no whore. The scene at the moated grange is often admired for its peaceful sweet sadness, its contrast with the flux and bawdiness of the play's "Vienna." Her five-year unrequited love fascinated Tennyson. Ladies in many stories have waited longer, but with Mariana the years are not just a cipher for "a long time." She is psychologically convincing in her fixation, and the scene gives her the moral weight she needs to play so major and so unforeseen a role in resolving the plot. In fact, she is brought on as yet another of the Duke's sharply tested subjects. When he arrives she stops the song of unrequited love she has ordered sung and calls him "a man of comfort, whose advice / Hath often still'd my brawling discontent" (4.1.8–9—the Duke has been visiting her in his Friar disguise even before devising the bed trick). She apologizes for appearing "so musical" and says of her song, "My mirth it much displeased, but pleased my woe." The Duke sympathizes, though he warns that music's affective powers must be applied with caution. Mariana is thus shown to suffer a form of love melancholy. Burton in *Anatomy of Melancholy* explains that for some love sufferers "the melody of musick, merriment, singing, dancing doth augment the passion" and thus that "These things must be warily applied, as the parties' Symptoms vary";

for other love sufferers, he notes, music is beneficial: though it makes them melancholy, "it is a pleasing melancholy that it causeth; and therefore to such as are discontent, in woe, fear, sorrow, or dejected, it is a most present remedy; it . . . easeth in an instant." Such a one is Mariana, feeding and nursing her melancholic love, beyond the time when it would naturally have died, with sad music that pleases and eases her woe, with isolation, and with religious exercises, thereby maintaining her obsession. The Duke sympathizes with her, and the bed trick with her beloved Angelo challenges her to renounce her seclusion, venture out of her moated country house, and enter the threatening world of the city. According to medical theory of the time, only such a proposition, integral to her obsession, could succeed. Thus the Duke tests Mariana, and she, like the provost, rises to the occasion.

As imitator of God the Duke may seem to have his finest moments in act 5, which the allegorizer sees as judgment day—and so it is, in the play's theological pattern. But here as earlier, the pattern works ironically. Anyone who thinks the play is straightforwardly doctrinal should try to imagine the scene of literal Judgment Day, where the most rebellious and deceitful of the goats can interrupt the proceedings repeatedly with bawdy, self-serving interjections that evoke from God only ineffectual chiding (Lucio's role). Here again, as when the Duke casts himself as absentee master and thereby attains the glory of usury, his self-image as imitator of God is humorous. His authority will not be destroyed, but it will be challenged, loudly and appealingly, until the end.

Throughout the play this challenging of the Duke's efforts to bring moral health to his subjects continues at almost regular intervals. Thus the theological pattern works dialectically, shaping a plot structure in which the Duke's moral point of view is asserted, then that of natural human drives, then the Duke's, then the contrary, and so on. After the Duke's opening pronouncements (1.1), 1.2 works entirely against his hopes, with Lucio's pirates erasing some of the Ten Commandments, Pompey's scornful view of Claudio's offense as "groping for trouts in a peculiar river," and Claudio's own denunciation of the judgment; 1.3 again gives the Duke the floor so that he can explain the motive for his abdication (to purge the evil his leniency has allowed to grow). The last scene of the first act (1.4) gives us Lucio's version of Claudio's deed (euphemistically put for Isabella) as simply natural and expected: "Your brother and his lover have embraced. / As those that feed grow full, as blossoming time . . ." (1.4.43–48). Act 2 opens with

Angelo asserting the strict morality that the Duke has apparently commissioned him to enforce, then brings on Elbow and the mock-trial scene with Pompey's impudent assertions that unless "your worship" means "to geld and splay all the youth of the city" then "Truly, sir, in my poor opinion, they will to't" and that "The valiant heart's not whipt out of his trade." This dialectic or alternation of opposed forces continues throughout the play, though not exactly scene for scene, since as complications increase each scene often has several functions.

The motion of the plot is thus tit for tat, measure for measure. The forces of natural human corruption, the "old man" of Pauline theology (Isabella desires Angelo to act with mercy, "like man new made"), give back blow for blow to the Duke's initiatives as a Christian ruler trying to imitate God. Claudio's challenge of his sentence (which the Duke so far accepts), Pompey's intransigence, Angelo's second betrayal (reaffirming the death sentence in breach of promise), which catches the Duke flat-footed, Barnardine's successful defiance of the Duke, Lucio's insults sticking to him "like a burr," and supremely Lucio's humorous interruptions of his so carefully contrived judgment day—these are the high points of this "dark" half of the plot, mostly very funny, but with a kind of *Galgen-humor* built on pervasive images of prostitution, venereal disease, groaning childbirth, hangovers, whipping, hanging, and beheading. After this battle of moral thesis and immoral antithesis, is there a final synthesis? No; the Duke wins, but on points—there is no knockout. And the losers will doubtless soon challenge again.

Measure for Measure was produced at court, in the year following King James's accession, and Bennett is surely right that it alludes to the king. The play responds in a careful and subtle fashion to his optimistic hopes that his ideals of Christian government would reform the body politic. We might presuppose that the ruler's stratagems ought to succeed with persons so well intentioned to start with as the play's major characters, especially since the ruler in the play had to emerge in control—who would risk defaming so Christian a ruler before so declaredly Christian a king? But Vienna retains its many "wicked villains despite of all grace." Lucio at the end is still his idle, cynical, profligate, deceitful, and amusing self, disadvantaged by a bad marriage. And he and Barnardine, who is simply released unchanged, together with Mrs. Overdone, her employees, and customers, stand for all the other loose characters of various social classes who will doubtless continue to ruin their minds and health with idleness, drunkenness, brawling, venereal disease, bad debts, and so on. The point is not that any judgment day must have some goats but that Shakespeare, while giving to the Duke and his morality the definition of the plot and the last word of judgment, nevertheless gives human evil so loud, so forceful, and at times so appealing a voice in the play—he allows it so to undermine the dignity, though not the power, of the ruler—that the controversy surrounding *Measure for Measure* may never end. For every critic who wants to emphasize grace, mercy, and the undoubted moral improvement of the major characters, there will be another who finds the Duke a meddler, the humor rancid, the marriages hollow. Tit for tat, measure for measure.

Would Shakespeare's audience have perceived the irony I have seen in the Duke's *imitatio dei* role? The play's chief antagonists are an ascetic, self-righteous Puritan and a naive papist proud of her good works (a novice nun); a benign, "temperate" ruler (3.2.237) intervenes to save them, as James I always hoped to do for the Puritans and Catholics not only of his own realm but of all Europe. The more thoughtful in the audience would have seen subtle ironies in this treatment of the ruler as imitator of God in judgment and mercy. In his famous and widely discussed "king's book," the *Basilikon Doron,* which sold thousands of copies in 1603, James had described the ruler as a "little God," a potentate "in the stile of Gods . . . Resembling right your mightie King Diuine." As in *The Trew Law of Free Monarchies* of his Scottish years, James throughout his reign recurred to the metaphor of the king as head of the body politic as Christ in the Pauline analogy is head of his body, the church. To Puritans, even to moderate ones who could conform to the Thirty-Nine Articles, James's versions of these topoi smacked of presumption, sometimes of blasphemy. Even a political moderate reports of a royal speech to Parliament "on the nature of Kingly power":

> his Majesty made them a Speech of two Hours long; wherein he shewed great Learning . . . only the most strictly religious could have wished that *his Highness would have been more spareing in using the Name of God, and comparing the Deity with Princes Soveraignty.*

Measure for Measure does not take any stand on the divine right of royal authority, though righteous versus corrupt authority is certainly one of its major themes. What I see as an ironic handling of the "little God" concept results from a succession of dark moments colored by several brief ironic allusions that were subtle enough to elude King James and his intimates while striking vibrations in the more perceptive of the court audience.

For there were many who saw, after only a year and a half of James's rule, that he would fall short of the lofty ideal in "the king's book." His lavish expenditures, his constant escape from matters of state in hunting, his rashness and theatricality in making decisions—typified by the famous gallows scene of condemning then at the last moment pardoning Markham, Grey, and Cobham in December 1603—such things were already on many tongues and in many letters. Nor could James, any more than could Duke Vincentio, remain unstung by "base calumniators." In short, given the controversies of the day, when many were questioning the concept of the ruler as divine image and arm, Shakespeare's audience could not have been impervious to ironic overtones on that point.

Bennett's idea of the Duke, especially in act 5, as a comic dramatist trying to press his characters into an order they stubbornly resist is illuminating. The Duke does indeed stage an elaborately planned playlet to dramatize the results Angelo's sins would have had if Angelo had had his way. The point is to make Angelo work through his guilt by seeing it in action and thereby truly repent and to give Mariana and Isabella their chance to experience, respectively, active loyalty and true forgiveness. In these aims the playlet succeeds, but not as planned. Lucio's final insolence in unmasking the "Friar" precludes whatever the Duke has memorized for his reappearance as Friar Lodowick and whatever he has planned for an ending. Henceforth the Duke must invent as he goes, and thus the often-noted awkwardness in his conclusion of the plot seems grounded in the situation: he is a man of many plans and preparations, forced to improvise.

Absorbed in his providential improvisations, the Duke has not had time to make the least preparation for a marriage between himself and Isabella. Yet now it is time for his playlet to end, and the marriage must simply be declared. It could have been prepared for. After what Isabella has learned she is a fine match for the Duke, and the idea of a nobleman testing and maturing a bride, choosing her with deliberation (rather than hastily while pierced "with the dribbling dart of love"), perhaps even rescuing her from nuns' vows, was a well-accepted motif on the English stage (cf. Robert Greene, *Friar Bacon and Friar Bungay*). Unfortunately the play has not explicitly reminded us of any of this, and the Duke's proposal surprises the audience just as much as it does

Isabella and leaves us equally unconvinced. Furthermore, the Duke's extended deception of Isabella about her brother's remaining alive (necessitated by his scheme for bringing her to charity and forgiveness), even though we know its worthy purpose, has cast a pall of cruel manipulation over his treatement of her that is inconsistent with his usual charity and kindliness (e.g., his efforts to console the prisoners before death, his comforting of Claudio and Isabella after their clash, his forebearance with Angelo, his praise of the provost's goodness, his comforting of Mariana). When Claudio appears Isabella would have to be at best dumbfounded at the Duke's actions and thus hardly in a mood to entertain his proposal.

The marriage of Angelo to Mariana can be accepted quite well if one believes in his repentance (which seems convincing, given his tortured conscience and the way one sin has let to another with him) and if one does not make the modern demand that both partners be in love. Lucio's marriage to Kate Keepdown is fitting as retributive justice and, dramatically, as deflation of a glorious liar, though it pains some people just as Falstaff's banishment does. Claudio's marriage at last to Juliet (who was in labor and "very near her hour" in 2.2, a day and a half ago, so must by now have delivered—she may appear holding the new baby) is unexceptionable if amusing as the ne plus ultra of the shotgun wedding. But the lack of preparation for the Duke's marriage proposal, seemingly a weakness in the play's dramatic structure, provides the greatest challenge to directorial ingenuity: both Isabella and the audience must somehow be brought to accept the proposal. That each of the four marriages is a form of moral correction for one or both partners (like sour-sweet medicine) entirely accords with the play's tone.

King James no doubt missed its "dark" side and saw a Christian ruler, standing for God in human government and, with some amusing incidents along the way, leading his salvageable subjects to improved moral stature while punishing those beyond help. So the play may be taken, and just so King James loved to picture himself. But by humorously questioning the Duke's authority, by making the bawds, whores, and fops more likable than most of the major characters, by harping on the inevitability of unlawful sex (which comes to stand for the chaotic, potentially destructive forces of human personality in society)—by doing these things Shakespeare has created a comedy with many ironic moments, which are usually stressed much more in modern productions than they could have been at King James's court.

Measure for Measure shows what a delicate balance exists between morality, the standards that generally make for mental and physical health as well as for reliable interaction within the body politic, and the potent drives of the "old man" that "will not die today for any man's persuasion," that will crop up even in the most ascetic personality, indeed especially there. The testing master delving beneath the surface must always be taken aback by his results, and even his best efforts to apply craft against vice will be undermined, interrupted, made laughable in their moment of success. In the world of the play people will always "play such fantastic tricks before high heaven / As makes the angels weep; who, with our spleens, / Would all themselves laugh mortal" (2.2.121–23). Is the play dark or not? Is it matter for weeping or laughing? It is both, though I believe Shakespeare meant act 5 to be played for all possible laughs.

While not regarding *Measure for Measure* as flawless or as one of Shakespeare's greatest plays, I believe that the Duke's character and role are carefully worked out, that the play's biblical and theological allusions do indeed evoke a parallel between the Duke and God, as testing master, redeemer, and judge, but that they function comically, to point up that he is not God but a ruler attempting *imitatio dei* in his government, with partly successful and sometimes humorous results. His quest for self-knowledge, his love of retirement and temperance (3.2.232–37), his talent for intrigue, and his efforts to bring moral improvement to his subjects clearly set him off from the other characters, and he should not be seen as hypocritical or neurotic.

Neither should he be elevated to divinity. Why must the play be either dark or sententious? Let it be a comedy of a well-intentioned ruler with the rather quixotic notion of actually imitating the New Testament God in his government. To the extent that the Duke depicts James I, he is less the real James than the virtuous, promising king as he appeared at the hopeful start of his reign in the bright mirror of his published writings—as if Shakespeare had said to himself, "All right, bring this image of a sincerely, actively Christian ruler to life, set him down in a normal, corrupt society, and observe the results." Directors should be able to give us such a Duke, who is learning to know his subjects as he has tried to know himself, a Duke who is human, sometimes a butt of humor, inclined to meddling and theatricality, sensitive to slander, yet self-aware, resourceful, charitable, and a judge of character. Such a measured approach might give us more of the richness of this much maligned and distorted play.

Measure for Measure
and the Art of Not Dying

Phoebe S. Spinrad

In many ways, Shakespeare's *Measure for Measure* may be considered a culmination of the Morality tradition that extends from *Pride of Life* to *Doctor Faustus*: a tradition that poses the moment of death as an understanding of life, offers the soul a last chance on earth to choose salvation or damnation, and dispatches the soul accordingly. But in *Measure for Measure,* the soul is not dispatched. And in this respect, Shakespeare's "problem" play mirrors the "problem" of life itself: that even though death offers the perfection of salvation to an imperfect world, we are often afraid to accept the terms of the offer; and that when we have overcome our fear and are ready to embrace death as a release, the kindly offer may be withdrawn.

This is not to suggest that *Measure for Measure* is a grim forerunner of the twentieth-century existentialist school, or that we are meant to leave the theater shaking our heads in pity over the bad fortune that has inflicted life upon the characters of the play. Claudio, Isabella, and Angelo, we feel—yes, and even Lucio and Pompey—will be as moderately happy with their lots as any human creatures can hope to be. But there *are* some grim sets of images that dominate the action of the play, of which the primary and most pervasive is that of the prison, both the literal prison of Vienna and the figurative prison of life.

The pivot of the action in *Measure for Measure* is, of course, Claudio's death sentence, and throughout all but the first and last scenes of the play, Claudio remains in prison. To this prison come the

From *Texas Studies in Literature and Language* 26, no. 1 (Spring 1984). © 1984 by the University of Texas Press.

Duke, Isabella, Lucio, and Pompey; in this prison reside the provost and Abhorson, the executioner; and ordering the affairs of this prison are Angelo and Escalus. Outside the prison walls are more walls: Isabella's convent, Mariana's moated grange, and Angelo's double-locked garden and chamber. By the end of the play, although some of the characters will elect to remain in their enclosures, or will exchange one enclosure for another, most of the original doors will be opened, and the inmates will be allowed to leave. What is interesting, however, is that each character will first come to realize that there are more ways out of prison than the one that he or she has planned, and that one of the doors is Death.

In several of the possible sources of Shakespeare's play, this alternate exit is indeed made the subject of a grim joke. Juriste, the Angelo-counterpart of Cinthio's *Epitia* (1582), also promises to free Epitia's brother from prison if she will go to bed with him; but after she has done so, Juriste sends her the dead body of her brother with a messenger who explains: "This . . . is your brother whom my lord Governor sends you freed from prison." In the play that Cinthio himself made from this story in the *Hecatomithi,* the joke becomes more elaborate; the messenger is made to deliver the message twice (once to the maid and once to Epitia), and Juriste's sister, Angela, explains the irony to the audience, who may have missed the point:

ANGELA: My brother I have cursed.

. . . .
He answered, that he promised Epitia
To give her Vico freed from prison, true,
But never promised to release him living;
So that she has exactly what he promised.
(3.2.)

In George Whetstone's *Promos and Cassandra* (1578), another promiser fulfills his pledge ironically. With the head sent to Cassandra, Promos sends a message that: "To Cassandra, as Promos promised thee, / From prison, lo, he sends thy brother free" (4.2). And in Thomas Lupton's *Too Good to Be True* (1581), although no such ghastly message is carried to the gentlewoman with her husband's body, the judge speaks in what appear to be deliberately equivocal terms: "and whereas your husband should have been executed tomorrow in the morning, I will dispatch him and send him home tomorrow unto you before noon at the furthest, if it be not before." The gentlewoman's husband is, of course, "dispatched" by the hangman.

Shakespeare omits this sadistic joke from his play—probably to make Angelo less evil and more forgivable. But the underlying irony of the joke is one that is inherent in a more serious tradition: the *de contemptu mundi* view of life itself as a prison and death as a release. A motif running through both Roman Catholic and Protestant Arts of Dying, it was first and most forcefully stated by Pope Innocent III in *De Miseria Condicionis Humane:*

> "Infelix homo, quis me liberabit de corpore mortis huius?" Certe non vult exire de carcere qui non vult exire de corpore, nam carcer anime corpus est.

> ["Unhappy man that I am, who will release me from the body of this death?" Surely, no man wishes to escape from prison who does not wish to escape from the body, for the body is a prison to the soul.]

And again, of the just man, Innocent says: "Sustinet seculum tanquam exilium, clausus in corpore tanquam in carcare" (2.18; "He endures the world as though he were in exile, locked up in his body as in a prison"). The 1576 translator of Innocent's treatise, H. Kirton, indeed editorializes further on the theme: "Beholde the lamentation of the silly soule, which would fayne be discharged out of prison. Whereof the Psalmist sayth thus. O lorde bring my soule out of captiuitie. There is no rest nor quietnesse in anye place heere in this world." And the translator of Petrus Luccensis's *Dialogue of Dying Wel* (trans. 1603) carries the analogy still further to Claudio's case:

> When an imprisoned malefactor hath receaued sentence of death and knoweth he cannot escape, oh how many waylings, and how many lamentings maketh the wretche in that time, seeing that assuredly he must foorthwith be put to death. In this case are all men liuing found to bee, against whome as soone as euer they be borne, in this miserable and transitorie lyfe, the seuere sentence of death is pronounced.

That such a motif had become almost a commonplace by the time of *Measure for Measure* is evident not only from its appearance in treatises, poems, and broadsides but also from the sardonic remark made by Sir Charles Mountford on his release from prison in Thomas

Heywood's *A Woman Killed with Kindness* (ca. 1603), a play whose subplot also requires that a sister sacrifice her honor for her brother's well-being:

> KEEPER: Knight, be of comfort, for I bring thee freedom
> From all thy troubles.
> SIR CHARLES: Then am I doom'd to die;
> Death is th' end of all calamity.

And in this sense of death as a release from prison, the famous act 3 prison scene of *Measure for Measure* may be considered a series of attempts by the Duke and Isabella to offer Claudio every possible escape route out of his prison, while Claudio obdurately refuses them all.

Shakespeare's audience would certainly have understood the Duke's "Be absolute for death" speech (3.1.5–41) as a compendium of many traditional Christian exhortations on the vanities of life—and if, as some critics have maintained, the speech contains allusions to such pagan philosophers as Lucretius, it is Lucretius filtered through Christian homiletics. Pope Innocent himself had used many of the figures and analogies that the Duke uses: the baseness of the flesh, the revolt of the organs of the body, and the afflictions that torment all living creatures regardless of age, class, or virtue. Treatise after treatise had echoed Innocent in these figures and had echoed as well his comparison of death to a welcome sleep, just as does the Duke:

> DUKE: Thy best of rest is sleep;
> And that thou oft provok'st, yet grossly fear'st
> Thy death, which is no more.
>
> (3.1.17–19)

But in order to welcome sleep, one must first be weary, and Claudio is by no means weary of his life. Consequently, the Duke, like the preachers before him, must first evoke in Claudio a sense of the frustrations in life:

> DUKE: Reason thus with life:
> If I do lose thee, I do lose a thing
> That none but fools would keep. A breath thou art,
> Servile to all the skyey influences
> That dost this habitation where thou keep'st
> Hourly afflict.
>
> (3.1.6–11)

This idea of the insubstantiality of human existence is certainly not contrary to Christian belief, as J. W. Lever has claimed; it does not deny the divine origin of the soul, but rather contrasts the soul's heavenly importance with the laughably frail, earthly shell in which the soul resides. E. Hutchins, in his popular and rather lovely religious handbook, *David's Sling against Goliath* (1598), had made many such comparisons about human life on earth:

> Now therefore reason with me. Shal we feare death for the losse of a shadow: shall wee by sighs and sobs storme againste the Lorde for the loss of a vapour? . . . So y^t our life is like a ruinous house, alwayes readie to fall: like a thin thred, alwaies readie to rotte: like a running cloude, whereof we are vncertaine, where and when it falleth.

Considering the downfall of Claudio's expectations, he should certainly be receptive to such preaching.

But unfortunately, weak, mortal creatures seldom respond as they should and, when subjected to uncertainties in life, usually assume that they can find compensating certainties in that same life. Such was Everyman's assumption; such is Claudio's. At first, it is true, he seems to have resigned himself to death and to be giving the theologically proper response: "To sue to live, I find I seek to die, / And seeking death, find life. Let it come on" (3.1.42–43). Christopher Sutton's *Disce Mori* (ca. 1600) had said much the same thing: "That which we call life, is a kinde of death, because it makes us to die: but that which we count death, is in the sequele a very life: for that in deede it makes us to live." Or, in Kirton's translation of *De Miseria*: "We then are dying whiles we liue, and then doe we cease from dying, when we cease to liue. Therefore it is better to dye, alwayes to liue, than to liue to dye euer. For the mortall lyfe of man is but a liuing death." For Claudio, so far, so good. But he and the audience know something that the Duke does not know: Isabella has been to see Angelo about Claudio's pardon and is even now on her way to the prison—to open, as Claudio thinks, an exit for him other than dying. As long as he retains this hope for another exit, he cannot be "absolute for death."

There is, furthermore, another element missing from Claudio's apparent preparation for death: repentance. The *de contemptu mundi* sermon which the Duke has given him was traditionally only the first step toward readying the dying man; it forms the first of three parts in Innocent's *De Miseria,* the other two of which deal with the deadly sins and the pains of hell; and it serves primarily as an introduction to the serious business of death in all the Arts of Dying. But the Duke does not have a chance to proceed to the second step of his deathbed counseling; he is interrupted by the arrival of Isabella. And from the moment Isabella enters, we know that Claudio has not really accepted the fact of death.

Claudio's first question—"Now, sister, what's the comfort?" (3.1.53)—is much like Everyman's questioning, in that it is posed in temporal rather than eternal terms; his "comfort," at this point, should be the ghostly comfort that the Duke has given, but Claudio speaks only in terms of life on earth. Isabella apparently senses his weakness and his excessive attachment to life at any cost. Although she has earlier assured herself that her brother would gladly die "On twenty bloody blocks" to save his soul and hers (2.4.176–82), his plea for "comfort" seems to frighten her into a circumlocution. Instead of blurting out Angelo's perfidy and the choice which Claudio must make, she spins an elaborate conceit on Claudio's coming journey to heaven, where he will be an "everlasting leiger," an ambassador in the court of God (3.1.56–60). It is noteworthy that she has omitted any mention of the words "die" and "death" and has inverted the traditional figure of "Death, the mighty messenger" to make Claudio the messenger instead.

But Claudio is still looking for a way out and, by a series of more and more insistent questions, forces his sister into telling him what he does not want to know:

> CLAUDIO: Is there no remedy?
> ISABELLA: None, but such remedy as, to save a head,
>   To cleave a heart in twain.
> CLAUDIO: But is there any?
>   (3.1.60–62)

The audience, here, might remember parts of the first debate between Angelo and Isabella, in which earthly and heavenly "remedies" were compared:

> ISABELLA: Must he needs die?
> ANGELO: Maiden, no remedy.
>   .   .   .   .
> ANGELO: Your brother is a forfeit of the law,
>   And you but waste your words.

> ISABELLA: Alas, alas!
> Why, all the souls that were, were forfeit once,
> And He that might the vantage best have took
> Found out the remedy.
>
> (2.3.48,71–75)

Why does Isabella not point out this heavenly "remedy" to Claudio? Perhaps because his mode of questioning has already indicated to her, as it has to us, that he is not open to heavenly comfort yet, that he is still too concerned with earthly comforts.

Isabella, then, becomes a shrewder comforter than the Duke has been, although she, too, will fail temporarily. Taking her cue from Claudio's questions, she turns not to the *de contemptu mundi* (which her brother will not believe) but to the Christian humanist's approach to death: the appeal to heroism and the integrity of the human spirit. She begins in the negative vein, evincing doubt about Claudio's courage— perhaps as a natural expression of her new fear, but also as a plea for Claudio to prove her wrong:

> ISABELLA: O, I do fear thee, Claudio, and I quake
> Lest thou a feverous life shouldst entertain,
> And six or seven winters more respect
> Than a perpetual honour. Dar'st thou die?
> The sense of death is most in apprehension,
> And the poor beetle that we tread upon
> In corporal sufferance finds a pang as great
> As when a giant dies.
>
> (3.1.73–80)

This is much like two of the arguments used by the Christian humanist Thomas Lupset in *A Compendious Treatise Teachynge the Waie of Dieyng Well* (1530): first, that it is just as foolish to haggle over a few years of life as it would be for a condemned felon to demand to approach the scaffold last in line; and second, that the pain of dying is of necessity a short one, feared more by beasts than by men. "Let vs then take a lusty courage of this desperation," Lupset had said, "seeinge there is no remedy: lette vs manfully go to it." And this ploy, for the moment, seems to work on Claudio. Flushed with resentment, he demands hotly, "Why give you me this shame?" And just as he has echoed the religious tone of the *de contemptu mundi* in reply to the Duke, so he echoes the heroic tone of Lupset's "good pagan" in reply to Isabella:

> CLAUDIO: If I must die,
> I will encounter darkness as a bride,
> And hug it in mine arms.
>
> (3.1.82–84)

Alas, alas, as Isabella would say. The sexual imagery and conditional "if" clause bode no good. But since Claudio has apparently responded to the humanist's call to honor, Isabella reinforces her appeal in the positive vein, congratulating him on his nobility and adding a confirmatory appeal to family as well as individual honor: "There spake my brother: there my father's grave / Did utter forth a voice" (3.1.85–86). Claudio, after all, as the eldest male in the family, *should* be willing to lay down his life for his sister's honor. But can there be some subliminal warning bell that causes her, even in the midst of her approving speech, to answer Claudio's "if" with such a positive "yes"? "Yes," she says, "thou must die" (3.1.86).

Claudio is still bargaining. To be sure, he can expect more than the "six or seven winters" which Isabella has predicted for him, and for a man still too firmly attached to this world to see things in terms of the next, even six or seven years seem better than six or seven hours. Perhaps he may even find a way, in those years, to redeem his honor—and his soul. But he is in the position, now, of Lupset's convict, merely dropping back a place in line each time the line moves toward the hangman; and every time he drops back, he makes death harder for himself.

Both the Duke and Isabella may indeed have misjudged the nature of Claudio's fear, or at least the nature of his worldly attachment. He is not merely clinging to the outward trappings of fashion, as the Duke has imagined; nor is he merely flying from the fear of corporal pain, as Isabella has imagined. Claudio is more pagan than either of his comforters has realized; he fears and half believes in the total annihilation of self. The first words of his last desperate appeal for life are a cry of horror at self-disintegration—a cry couched solely in terms of the body, the only self he knows:

> CLAUDIO: Aye, but to die, and go we know not where;
> To lie in cold obstruction, and to rot;
> This sensible warm motion to become
> A kneaded clod
>
> (3.1.117–20)

The very words of the *de contemptu mundi* have become, for Claudio, not a reason to prepare for death but a reason to dread it.

When Claudio turns his mind to the possibility of an afterlife, he is perhaps not quite pagan, but not quite an ideal Christian either. He gives no thought to heaven, but pictures in turn the fires of the preachers' hell and the torments of Dante's Inferno: the "thick-ribb'd ice" of the traitors and the windblown eternal motion of the uncommitted and the lustful. All his thoughts are of dissolution, agony, and damnation; he has succumbed at once to the traditional deathbed temptations of infidelity, impatience, and despair.

In such a state of mind, Claudio may well cry out, with Hamlet, that the suffering of life may be preferable to the sleep of death, that "the dread of something after death" (in Claudio's case, perhaps, the dread of Nothing after death) "makes us rather bear the ills we have / Than fly to others that we know not of" (*Hamlet,* 3.1.78–82):

> CLAUDIO: The weariest and most loathed worldly life
> That age, ache, penury, and imprisonment
> Can lay on nature, is a paradise
> To what we fear of death.
>
> (3.1.128–31)

He cannot now believe the preachers who have tried to tell him the opposite: "Yea, this case of the soule is such a cage of filth, as a man of God hath said, that no Bocardo, no dungeon, no sinke, no puddle, no pitte is in any respect so evil a prison for this bodie, as the bodie is of the soule."

This is not to suggest that Claudio is wrong to fear death; no preacher or poet would have claimed that such fear is unnatural. But all would have remarked upon Claudio's failure to overcome his fear, whether by faith or by reason, and would especially have pointed out that to bargain for life at the expense of one's soul is a mortal sin: "Saynt Austyn sayth: More greate is the dommage of one soule the which is loste and deed by dampnacyon than it is of yᵉ dethe of a thousande bodyes deed of the dethe corporall and by putryfaccyon." How much worse, then, to bargain for life at the expense of someone else—a deed that will encompass the "dampnacyon" of not one, but two immortal souls.

Claudio, however, is beyond the reach of traditional appeals. He is a Worldly Man in a sense undreamed of by the sixteenth-century Moralists: the man who sees Nothing beyond the limits of his own consciousness, the quasi-solipsist who in his own demise sees the disappearance of the universe. Both the medieval and the Renaissance Christian formulas are therefore meaningless to him, since both posit a universe independent of his own being; for him to accept death, he must be convinced of the existence of things outside himself, of a continuity of Being once he is gone. And Isabella, whose impulsiveness so often bursts out in wild and whirling words, in her own desperation hits upon the right cure for her brother:

ISABELLA: O you beast!
O faithless coward! O dishonest wretch!
    Wilt thou be made a man out of my vice?

    .   .   .   .

                         Take my defiance,
    Die, perish! Might but my bending down
    Reprieve thee from thy fate, it should proceed.
    I'll pray a thousand prayers for thy death;
    No word to save thee.
                                    (3.1.135–37, 142–46)

It is an angry speech, a furious speech, a violent rush of words from a young woman at the end of her rope. And almost from the earliest performances of *Measure for Measure,* critics have either denounced the speech or made tortuous excuses for it. But ironically, the one thing that both Isabella's detractors and her champions have glossed over too quickly in their analyses of her words is the most important thing about them: they work where all else has failed.

Up to now, Claudio has managed to control his universe, despite the sentence of death, and has thus managed to maintain his sense of being the universe. He has sent for his sister, and his sister has arrived. He has tossed off the correct response to the Duke's sermon, and the Duke has been satisfied. He has juggled with the seven deadly sins to make Angelo's proposition seem sinless, and he has convinced himself and fully expects to convince his sister. Even the apparent coincidence that the "precise" Angelo should suddenly act out of character in a way that may save Claudio's life is proof that Claudio's will makes and remakes the universe. How, then, should he die?

The only answer is Isabella's. Her defiance, her thrusting of death in his face when he has it least in mind, her very refusal to listen to his repeated cries of "Oh, hear me, Isabella!" are all concrete evidence of a world outside Claudio's control. And Claudio, who has declared himself unafraid of "age, ache, penury, and imprisonment," is shocked back to reality by something far worse than any of them: a sister's contempt.

To be sure, his immediate response to Isabella's outburst is no more promising than was his response to the Duke's sermon, or to Isabella's first appeal: "I am so out of love with life that I will sue to be rid of it" (3.1.170–71). We have heard those words before, and then have heard Claudio retract them. But his preface to them, this time, *is* promising: "Let me ask my sister pardon." Theologically, he has taken the first step toward repentance, and psychologically, he has taken the first step toward acceptance: he has admitted that there is Being outside himself, and at least a human being, if not a divine one, more important than himself.

The results of Isabella's shock treatment become most evident later in the play, when Claudio and Barnardine are served their death warrants. Claudio now evinces a calm acceptance of his mortality, and when asked about Barnardine, uses a simile which links his own past with Barnardine's present: "As fast locked up in sleep as guiltless labor / When it lies starkly in the traveller's bones" (4.2.64–65). Despite the implicit irony of the word "guiltless" (Claudio is not above sarcasm himself), this is not the traditional metaphor of sleep as a type of corporal death, but rather a metaphor which the Duke has introduced earlier: sleep as a type of spiritual death—an insensibility to the meanings of life and death alike: "Thou hast nor youth, nor age, / But as it were an after-dinner's sleep / Dreaming on both" (3.1.32–34). The provost himself sees Barnardine in these terms: "A man that apprehends death no more dreadfully but as a drunken sleep" (4.2.140–41). And when Barnardine receives his summons to death, he flatly refuses to die.

In the old Morality plays, and even in the new secular tragedies, Barnardine would have had no choice. Humanum Genus and Everyman at first refused to die; Tamburlaine and Macbeth refused to die; and all of them died. Why Barnardine is allowed his refusal we shall see later; but the refusal itself, at this point, serves as an almost allegorized extension of Claudio's previous denial and bargaining, and thus throws his present acceptance into sharper relief. Indeed, the connection between the two men is reinforced by the nature of Barnardine's imprisonment, a form of transitional half-life similar to his "drunken sleep." He is the prisoner who cannot and will not be released to life or death; he has gained stay after stay of execution, and, the provost says, if he were offered a chance to escape, he would not go. Like Claudio, he prefers the circumscribed prison of his own ordering, where, by denying the power of forces outside himself, he can maintain the semblance of control. Does he not have "the liberty of the prison" (4.2.145–46)? But it is a prison after all.

The Duke's evaluation of Barnardine's insensibility—"Unfit to live or die. O gravel heart!" (4.3.63)—is, then, a commentary on Claudio's earlier behavior as well. But as always in this play where people say much more than they think they mean, the Duke is speaking not just of Barnardine and Claudio but of all the major figures who move around him in prisons of their own making—including himself.

Like Claudio in his physical and mental prison, Angelo, Isabella, and the Duke begin by thinking that they can order the universe to their own requirements. Angelo in particular is the Puritan mind carried to its coldest extremes, a man who has mentally segregated humankind into the all-good and the all-bad, with no room in his world for the mixed creature who can sin, repent, and sin and repent again. But although—or perhaps because—he so easily sends the reprobate to a literal prison, he does not see that he is creating a separate but equal figurative prison for the elect.

Raymond Southall has postulated Angelo as an extreme post-Reformation Catholic type who relies too much on outward signs of grace, and Isabella as an extreme Protestant who relies too much on inward, individual signs; both, says Southall, must recombine into "Medieval Christianity." But such an interpretation seems curiously perverse—or at least makes Shakespeare seem curiously perverse in his methods. Why, after all, clothe a symbol of radical Protestantism in a nun's habit, unless to confuse the audience needlessly? And why refer to a Roman Catholic as "precise" (1.3.50), a term used almost exclusively of Puritans in Shakespeare's day? Indeed, Shakespeare's audience might have recognized Angelo as a Puritan even without references to his "precision" and would certainly have recognized the dangerous nature of his Puritanism: the frighteningly sincere distinction between good and evil that allows for no compromise and will make no exceptions, even for oneself.

To speak of Angelo's sincerity might sound as self-contradictory as to speak of Iago's honesty. But Isabella is only partly correct, during the judgment scene, when she says, "I partly think / A due sincerity govern'd his deeds / Till he did look on me" (5.1.443–45). A due, if warped, sincerity has governed Angelo's deeds even *after* he has looked on Isabella; he is as sincere in his sin as he was in his virtue. It is especially interesting to watch him chart his moral regression throughout the play and to match the chart against the Calvinist preacher William Perkins's outline of the progress of sin:

> Actuall sinne in the first degree of *tentation,* is, when the mind upon some sudden motion, is drawne away to thinke evill, and withall is tickled with some delight thereof. For a bad motion cast into the mind, by the flesh and the devill, is like unto the baite cast into the water, that allureth and delighteth the fish, and causeth it to bite. Sinne in *conception,* is when with the delight of the mind, there goes consent of the will to do the evill thought on. Sinne in *birth,* is when it comes forth into an action of execution. Sinne in *perfection,* is when men are growne to a custome and habite in sinne, upon long practice. . . . And sinne thus made perfect, brings foorth death.

In Angelo's first stage, temptation, he does indeed use the image of the bait and fish: "O cunning enemy, that, to catch a saint, / With saints dost bait thy hook!" (2.2.180–81). And when he has failed to master his temptation, he speaks of his "conception":

> ANGELO: Heaven in my mouth,
> As if I did but only chew his name,
> And in my heart the strong and swelling evil
> Of my conception.
>
>   (2.4.4–7)

Even his shocking double entendre to Isabella, "Plainly conceive, I love you" (2.4.140), may carry more than double meaning in this sense; he is inviting Isabella to give consent of her will to sin. And by the time he tells her, in no uncertain terms, "Fit thy consent to my sharp appetite" (2.4.160), he has looked ahead to the next stages of his sin: "I have begun, / And now I give my sensual race the rein" (2.4.158–59). He is predicting, here, not merely the birth, or action, of the sin of fornication, but perfection in sin, the next sin that he will "perform in the necke of" the first—lying to cover his tracks: "Say what you can, my false o'erweighs your true" (2.4.169).

Having charted his course so accurately, he must now expect that his "sinne thus made perfect, brings foorth death." And indeed, when we next see him alone, he explains in soliloquy that his reason for ordering Claudio's execution, in violation of his promise, was not gratiuitous villainy, but an attempt to stave off retribution for a while:

> ANGELO: He should have liv'd;
> Save that his riotous youth, with dangerous sense,
> Might in the times to come have ta'en revenge
> By so receiving a dishonor'd life
> With ransom of such shame. Would yet he had lived.
>
> (4.4.26–30)

That last phrase is a telling one. Angelo, knowing that he deserves death, half craves the punishment—but fears the consequences. For him, in his state of sin, death means hell.

From the beginning of the play, Angelo has served as his own prosecutor, judge, and jury. He sincerely believes what he has told Escalus:

> ANGELO: When I that censure him do so offend,
> Let mine own judgement pattern out my death,
> And nothing come in partial.
>
> (2.1.29–31)

When he does "so offend," then, he convicts himself utterly, leaving no room for a repentance that he, as a reprobate, cannot expect to be granted. Consequently, although he dreads the damnation that he knows will follow death, when his sins are exposed during the judgment scene, he twice demands his right to die—almost, we feel, with a touch of relief that the flight from death is over:

> ANGELO: Immediate sentence then, and sequent death
> Is all the grace I beg.
>
> .   .   .   .
>
> I am sorry that such sorrow I procure,
> And so deep sticks it in my penitent heart
> That I crave death more willingly than mercy;
> 'Tis my deserving, and I do entreat it.
>
> (5.1.371–72, 472–75)

Before we applaud Angelo's self-judgment, however, we must remember that a "penitent heart" does not refuse grace, mercy, or a chance to amend. This is not acceptance of death, but something uglier: despair. Isabella may forgive him; Mariana may forgive him; the Duke and all the laws of man and God may forgive him; but unless something drastic happens, Angelo will never forgive himself. Like Barnardine refusing to escape from jail, Angelo is locked into the prison of his rigid, ultra-Puritan belief: once a sinner, forever damned.

Isabella herself, who stands in opposition to Angelo throughout the play, opposes him only in the sense that a mirror image opposes the thing it reflects. She, too, wants to order the universe. Her idea of order, however, leans more to an ideal of neatness than to a system of rectitude; she is far more willing than Angelo to make moral exceptions for other people and is not above special pleading for a cause which she does not wholeheartedly espouse. It is especially noteworthy that when she learns that her brother has impregnated Juliet, her immediate response is not moral horror but commonsense practicality: "O, let him marry her" (1.4.49). But although she grants human society the right to go to hell happily on the road of its own choosing, she herself wants a divorce from that society and would choose for herself a martyr's crown—and a martyr's isolation.

There is no need to condemn the whole system of monasticism, or to assume, as Darryl F. Gless has recently done, that Shakespeare is condemning it, in order to see the self-imprisoning nature of Isabella's choices. She is not content with the already severe restrictions placed on the Poor Clares, whom she seeks to join, but would have the whole order translated into an ideal society of martyrs, one which probably cannot exist among fallible human creatures:

> ISABELLA: And have you nuns no farther privileges?
> NUN: Are not these large enough?
> ISABELLA: Yes, truly; I speak not as desiring more,
> But rather wishing a more strict restraint
> Upon the [sisterhood], the votarists of Saint Clare.
> (1.4.1–5)

Whether Lucio is indeed "mocking" her when he calls her "a thing enskied and sainted" (1.4.34) is a moot point; the important point is that Isabella would like to see her chosen world in these terms and that she finds it difficult to accept the existence of her own noble thoughts in the mind—or on the lips—of an ignoble creature from the outside world.

There is no reason, then, to doubt Isabella's word when she twice offers to lay down her life for her brother. It is the heroic thing to do, and Isabella yearns to be a saintly hero. The very words that she uses about her voluntary martyrdom show that she has adopted her ideas about sacrifice from the luridly detailed martyrologies of the time, as well as from the combined sensual and spiritual imagery of Loyolan meditation and the new poetry:

> ISABELLA: [W]ere I under the terms of death,
> Th' impression of keen whips I'd wear as rubies,
> And strip myself to death as to a bed
> That longing have been sick for, ere I'd yield
> My body up to shame.
>
> (2.4.100–105)

But Isabella is not now in the ideal world of the martyrologies, and her imagery only whets Angelo's sensual appetite. Furthermore, not even the audience is allowed to retain Isabella's romantic view; we are made too vividly aware that those "keen whips" are in the hands of the rough-hewn Abhorson and the bumbling Pompey, an ex-pimp.

Nothing goes the way Isabella expects. Angelo turns her brilliant logic-chopping against her; the noble Law makes illicit propositions; her glorious martyrdom must be traded for a sordid tumble; and her valiant brother, who should rush to her protection, turns out to be a sniveling coward. It is small wonder that when the Duke greets her after her disastrous interview with Claudio, she can hardly wait to get back to her nice, safe convent. "I have no superfluous leisure," she says. "My stay must be stolen out of other affairs; but I will attend you awhile" (3.1.156–58). This is no mere social excuse; Isabella has found the world too disappointing—yes, even too messy—and wants only to return as soon as possible to her ideal world where there are (she thinks) no loose ends and no human frailties.

It is exactly at this point that the Duke steps in and begins arranging the "happy" denouement. As Rosalind Miles, who perhaps unconsciously uses the prison metaphor in her analysis, points out:

> With this structure of character and plot involving Isabella, Angelo, and Claudio, the audience comes to realize that there is no help for these three from each other. Shakespeare has closed the trap of the plot upon them, and it is a trap which can only be opened from the outside. They must have external help, and that help must be the Duke's.

It is true; we do feel that there is, at this point, no way out but a guilty life or death for the three. But the "trap" of which Miles speaks is Shakespeare's only at second remove, and each of the characters has come to the trap through the mental trap each has built for himself or herself. Furthermore, the Duke's "external help" is itself a product of his own mental prison.

Miles's observation that the Duke's "outside intervention is bound to be artificial and unreal" is a good one, but again it focuses too much on Shakespeare's plot making at the expense of the Duke's. The Duke, after all, could just as easily have revealed himself at this point and saved the three in a more straightforward manner. But he, too, is circumscribed by a need to order the universe—a need that combines the active meddling impulse of Angelo with the passive withdrawal impulse of Isabella. From such a mixture can come only disaster.

From the beginning of the play, it is obvious that the Duke has been an anti-Machiavel, a ruler who wants to be loved more than feared by his subjects, and who has consequently been both too removed from and too permissive toward the people of Vienna. He has "ever lov'd the life removed," he tells Friar Thomas (1.3.8), but his failure to become more involved with the punitive aspects of his ducal responsibility has caused sin to run riot in Vienna. Friar Thomas's commonsense reply to this— "It rested in your Grace / To unloose this tied-up justice when you pleas'd" (1.3.31–32)—is not, however, to the Duke's liking. He pleads that it will seem "tyranny" in him to enforce the laws that he has previously ignored and, in a revealing bit of rationalization, explains why he has given that chore to Angelo:

> DUKE: I have on Angelo impos'd the office,
>   Who may in th' ambush of my name strike home,
>   And yet my nature never in the fight
>   To do in slander.
>
> (1.3.40–43)

We may recognize here the sentiments of every official, major or minor, down to the present day: the desire to be loved as a beneficent figure and a source of recourse against one's own rigorous enforcement agencies.

But things do not go according to plan for the Duke, any more than they do for Angelo, Isabella, or Claudio. Like the eavesdropping kings and queens of Shakespeare's history plays before him, the Duke discovers that his people do not universally applaud him, and he must listen to some unpleasant truths about himself even from the most slanderous tongues.

And what of the famous bed trick? It is indeed "artificial and unreal," as Miles has said, and so flimsy that we can hardly imagine Isabella agreeing to it if it had not been endorsed by a Friar. Furthermore, at the introduction of the bed trick, the play begins to change with an audible creaking of machinery. But there is one thing about the bed trick that has been consistently overlooked by critics who condemn it; the bed trick does not work.

In the tales and plays that used the trick before *Measure for Measure,* the ploy does what it is supposed to do: it brings about recognition, reconciliation, or revenge. Even in Shakespeare's own *All's Well That Ends Well,* Helena gets the man she wants through a bed trick—regardless of what we think about the scoundrel that she gets. But in *Measure for Measure,* the trick makes everything worse: it hastens the order for Claudio's execution, temporarily blackens the reputations of both Isabella and Mariana, and throws Angelo into a dangerous state of despair. The Duke himself is placed in a quandary by Angelo's response to the trick; he must suddenly change all his plans, must find a new way to save Claudio's life and Barnardine's soul, must very nearly reveal himself to the provost ahead of schedule, and must later subject himself and the two women to public scorn. What has gone wrong?

The men and women of *Measure for Measure,* when they assemble at the judgment scene, have wrought havoc with their own lives, with the lives of others, and with the storybook ending that we expect of a comedy. There have been too many playwrights at work within the play, each working from a script that the others have not seen. Even after the final revelations and pardons, many of them seem only to have left one prison for another. Mariana has come out of her moated grange to be tied for life to the puritanical Angelo. Angelo himself is in a state of despair that leads only to hell. Isabella, after what she has undergone, is as firmly locked out of her convent as she was once locked in. The Duke must abandon his own quasimonastic dreams to undertake marriage and the resumed rule of Vienna. Pompey has moved from the whorehouse to the executioner's shed. Barnardine, in or out of prison, remains in his "drunken sleep." And Lucio is married to a prostitute. Nothing, it seems, has changed, except possibly for the worse. Or has it?

The falloff which so many audiences have seen in the second part of Shakespeare's play is a reflection of the falloff which his characters have seen in their ideal worlds, as they learn to accept both death and life—their own and others'. And as in *Everyman* and the Arts of Dying, the central event of Claudio's death sentence has taught the lesson. Death, far from being the glorious martyrdom of Isabella's dreams, the comfortable sleep of the Duke's dreams, the nuisance of Barnardine's, the punishment of Angelo's, or the horror of Claudio's, is in fact simply a part of life, to be accepted on its own terms and neither fled from nor sought after. The readiness, as Hamlet would say, is all; and the readiness itself casts a steadier light on life, revealing that it cannot be perfect but must not therefore be scorned. If life, in fact, is second best to heaven or whatever perfection each person imagines as his or her own ideal, second best to perfection is not a lowly status after all.

This, then, is why Angelo and Barnardine must not be allowed to die. Theologically, they have not achieved repentance, and psychologically, they have not yet learned to live. In the end, what Mariana has said of Angelo is the lesson that all the great but fallible human creatures of *Measure for Measure* are in the process of learning about existence as they leave us:

> MARIANA: They say best men are molded out of faults,
> And, for the most, become much more the better
> For being a little bad. So may my husband.
>
> (5.1.444–46)

Death, as Sir Charles Mountford has said, is the end of all calamity—but in the words of the old Jewish proverb, "You don't die so easy; you live with all your aches and pains." The universe itself is a compromise of warring elements, and it is only through a truce with death that we may begin to negotiate with life.

"Instruments of Some More Mightier Member": The Constriction of Female Power in *Measure for Measure*

Marcia Riefer

Isabella has recently been called *Measure for Measure*'s "greatest problem." She has not always been taken so seriously. Coleridge dismissed her by saying simply that Isabella "of all Shakespeare's female characters, interests me the least." Criticism of her character has been cyclical and paradoxical, in part because critics have tended to focus on one implicit question: is she or is she not an exemplar of rectitude? On the one hand, Isabella has been idealized as a paragon of feminine virtue; on the other hand, she has been denigrated as an example of frigidity. Over the centuries, Isabella has been labeled either "angel" or "vixen," as if a judgment of her moral nature were the only important statement to be made about her. When not idealizing or denigrating Isabella, critics have generally ignored her.

I

The debate over Isabella's virtue obscures a more important point, namely that through her one can explore the negative effects of patriarchal attitudes on female characters and on the resolution of comedy itself. In the course of the play, Isabella changes from an articulate, compassionate woman during her first encounter with Angelo (2.2),

From *The Shakespeare Quarterly* 35, no. 2 (Summer 1984). © 1984 by the Folger Shakespeare Library.

to a stunned, angry, defensive woman in her later confrontations with Angleo and with her imprisoned brother (2.4 and 3.1), to, finally, a shadow of her former articulate self, on her knees before male authority in act 5. As the last and one of the most problematic of the preromance comedies, *Measure for Measure* traces Isabella's gradual loss of autonomy and ultimately demonstrates, among other things, the incompatibility of sexual subjugation with successful comic dramaturgy.

The kind of powerlessness Isabella experiences is an anomaly in Shakespearean comedy. Most of the heroines in whose footsteps Isabella follows have functioned as surrogate dramatist figures who are generally more powerful, in terms of manipulating plot, than the male characters in the same plays. One need only recall the Princess of France and her ladies in *Love's Labor's Lost,* Portia in *The Merchant of Venice,* Mistresses Page and Ford in *The Merry Wives of Windsor,* Beatrice in *Much Ado about Nothing,* Viola in *Twelfth Night,* Helena in *All's Well That Ends Well,* and, of course, Rosalind in *As You Like It.* Those heroines who have not actually been in control of the comic action have at least participated in it more actively than Isabella ever does. In *A Midsummer Night's Dream,* for instance, Helena and Hermia, while admittedly acting within Oberon's master plot, still take the initiative in pursuing their loves, which is certainly not true of Isabella. Even Kate in *The Taming of the Shrew* exercises dramaturgical skills. In her final "tour de force" she employs those very tactics which Petruchio has taught her, reversing them subtly on him and indicating through loving opposites—as he has done in his "taming" of her—that she may have some taming of her own in store for him. Her "obedience" to Petruchio's dramatic manipulation is far more playful and even assertive than Isabella's obedience to Vincentio. Besides, as Richard Wheeler points out, Petruchio's long-range significance is that the model of love by male conquest he embodies very soon drops out of the maturing world of Shakespeare's comedy, to be replaced by such forceful, loving heroines as Portia and Rosalind.

It is hardly incidental that in *Measure for Measure* Shakespeare places dramaturgical control almost exclusively in the hands of a male character—Duke Vincentio—who is, in effect, a parody of his more successful, mostly female, predecessors. An understanding of Vincentio's function in this play is essential background for exploring Isabella's character and dramatic function, so it is to him that we must turn our attention first.

II

As a dramatist figure, the Duke perverts Shakespeare's established comic paradigm in that he lacks certain essential dramaturgical skills and qualities previously associated with comic dramatist figures—qualities necessary for a satisfying resolution of comedy—especially (1) a consistent desire to bring about sexual union, what Northrop Frye calls "comic drive," and (2) a sensitivity to "audience." The prime victim of the Duke's flawed dramaturgy is, of course, Isabella, who, more than any of Shakespeare's heroines so far, is excluded from the "privileges of comedy," namely the privileges of exercising control over the events of the plot—privileges from which, Linda Bamber claims, it is Shakespeare's men who are typically excluded. Deprived of her potential for leadership, Isabella succumbs to the control of a man she has no choice but to obey—a man whose orders are highly questionable—and as a consequence her character is markedly diminished.

That the Duke's actions are questionable is apparent from the beginning, when he unexpectedly appoints Angelo to rule in his place instead of Escalus, who, as the opening scene establishes, is clearly the logical choice. Throughout the play, the Duke continues to undermine his credibility as a dramatist figure by making decisions strictly according to his own desires without considering the responses of those he is attempting to manipulate. For instance, his lofty tone in lecturing Claudio on how to make himself "absolute for death" (3.1.5–41) is far from sensitive to the condemned man's situation. Not surprisingly, his effort fails; within a hundred lines Claudio is begging, "Sweet sister, let me live" (1.132). Similarly unsympathetic, and similarly unsuccessful, is the Duke's attempt to convince the recalcitrant Barnardine to offer his head in place of Claudio's. This attempt results in the ridiculous appearance of a head whose owner, Ragozine, has no other purpose in the play than to cover for (even while calling attention to) Vincentio's insensitivity to the exigencies of motivation. The Duke's ineptitude as a playwright surrogate lies partly in his failure, in Viola's words, to "observe their mood on whom he jests" (*Twelfth Night,* 3.1.62)—a failure which will prove especially detrimental to Isabella.

Another way in which the Duke perverts the Shakespearean comic paradigm is in his unusual antagonistic relationship to the "normal action" of comedy which Frye defines as the struggle of the main characters to overcome obstacles in order to achieve sexual union. The Duke *appears* to be possessed by a comic drive toward union when he proposes the bed-trick (dubious as it is) or when he arranges what Anne Barton refers to as the "outbreak of that pairing-off disease" in act 5. But his explicit denial that he has anything in common with those sinners and weaklings who allow themselves to be struck by the "dribbling dart of love" (1.3.2)—along with his implicit condoning of Angelo's revival of obsolete sexual restrictive policies ("I have on Angelo impos'd the office, / Who may, in th' ambush of my name, strike home" [1.3.40–41])—sets him apart from earlier comic dramatists, predominantly women, whose desire was to escape, rather than to impose, sexual restriction. As Wheeler says, "*Measure for Measure* is guided to its comic conclusion by a character whose essence is the denial of family ties and sexuality, the denial, that is to say, of the essence of comedy." Vincentio represents not love's facilitator but its "blocking" agent. In this play, the hero and the "alazon" figure—the main obstacle to resolution in a typical comedy—are, ironically, identical. Thus, the Duke, as protagonist, also embodies those traits characteristic of a comic antagonist. The "savior" in *Measure for Measure* turns out to be a villain as well. (Vincentio even allies himself with the play's more obvious antagonist, announcing that Angelo can "my part in him advertise" [1.1.41] and inviting Angelo, in his absence, to be "at full ourself" [1.1.43]. The Duke's intent may be to flatter Angelo with these phrases, but by positing this unity of their characters, he leaves himself open to suspicion.)

Part of what is comically "villainous" in the Duke is his excessive self-interest. Thomas Van Laan is among those critics who point out the Duke's egotism, arguing that he "cares about his image above all else." Van Laan describes the Duke as writer/producer/director of his own "carefully devised playlet," a man who is "like some film star more interested in his own virtuosity than ideal representation of the script." Indeed, the Duke's purpose for relinquishing his public responsibilities—a purpose he himself admits is "grave and wrinkled" (1.3.5)—is reminiscent of Tom Sawyer's reason for playing dead: he wants to find out what people will say about him when he's gone.

While some may argue that such an evaluation of the Duke as selfishly motivated is unduly harsh, there is much in this play to support it, especially in those scenes in which the Duke's actions seem well-intentioned. During the opening scene, for example, Vincentio lavishes praise on Angelo in an unnecessarily long and rhetorically elaborate passage (1.1.26–41), all the while knowing that Angelo has abandoned Mariana, an act which the Duke later calls "unjust" (3.1.240). Far from having Vienna's best interests in mind as he claims—and as many critics accept—the Duke is actually setting up Angelo for a fall while protecting himself ("my nature never in the fight / To do in slander" [1.3.42–43]), and at the same time betraying the public as well, a public whom he admits he has effectively "bid" to be promiscuous through his permissiveness (2.36–38). His ultimate intention seems to be setting the stage for his final dramatic saving of the day—a day which would not need saving except for his contrivances in the first place. Vincentio's brand of dramaturgy is not as well-meaning as it first appears, and it should make us apprehensive about the Duke's potential to warp the experiences of those involved in his plots.

III

The female characters in this play, Mariana and Isabella, are the prime victims of the Duke's disturbing manipulativeness—a significant reversal of the roles women have played in earlier comedies. While both male and female characters serve to some extent as the Duke's "puppets," only the men resist his orders; the women are bound to be "directed" by him (4.3.136), "advised" by him (4.6.3), "rul'd" by him (4.6.4). As Jean E. Howard points out, Barnardine, Lucio, and Angelo, even though punished in the end, do at times "refuse to be pawns in someone else's tidy playscript": Barnardine refuses to die, Angelo refuses to pardon Claudio, Lucio refuses to shut up. Neither Mariana nor Isabella ever exhibits such defiance. Thus, this play creates a disturbing and unusual sense of female powerlessness. But far from prescribing female reticence, *Measure for Measure* serves to reveal contingencies that make it difficult for women, even strong-willed women like Isabella, to assert themselves in a patriarchal society like Vienna— contingencies that do not impinge in the same way on the men. By allowing such contingencies to dominate the action, Shakespeare throws into question both the play's status as a comedy and the legitimacy of the prevailing social standards it portrays.

When we judge Isabella, we must consider, as Wheeler does, that she is surrounded by "the threat of sexual degradation"—a threat which, in this play, is "moved to the very center of the comic action," while in the festive comedies that threat is "deflected by wit and subordinated to the larger movements" of those plays. More than any comic heroine thus far, Isabella has reason to take sexual degradation seriously. Whereas in most Shakespearean comedies the patriarchal world is peripheral to the main action, thereby allowing female characters exceptional latitude, in this play the expansiveness of a "green world" is inconceivable. Isabella has no Arden to retreat to. As Frye suggests, the green world in *Measure for Measure,* if present at all, has shrunk to the size of Mariana's all but inconsequential moated grange.

The constriction of the heroine's power throughout the course of Shakespeare's preromance comedies has been noted by Anthony Dawson, but only with regard to Portia, Rosalind, and Helena. Isabella represents the logical extension of this trend. The restrictiveness of Isabella's environment in *Measure for Measure* is evident in her doubts about her effectiveness ("My power? Alas, I doubt—" [1.4.77]) in the world as it must appear to her—a Vienna in which lust is rampant and in which even fiancées and wives are referred to in the same terms as whores. Elbow's speeches, for instance, denigrate, if inadvertently, his own wife: "My wife, sir, whom I detest before heaven and your honor—" (2.1.69–70), and "Marry, sir, by my wife, who, if she had been a woman cardinally given, might have been accus'd in fornication, adultery, and all uncleanliness there" (2.79–81). Of the female characters who appear in this play, none are actually wives, and the one who is betrothed, Juliet, is called a "fornicatress" (2.2.23). Otherwise, one of the women has been wronged (Mariana), one is a nun who has withdrawn from this lust-infected Vienna, one is trying to withdraw (Isabella), and the last is a whore (Mistress Overdone, nicknamed Madam Mitigation) whose customers are all sent to jail, leaving her to fret over her lost income. Sex in this Vienna is to be either punished or belittled. While Claudio, the true lover, sits in prison, the rakish Lucio roams the streets, joking about getting caught at a game of "tick-tack" (1.2.190–91). The word "healthy" could hardly be associated with female sexuality in such an environment, no matter how positively a woman saw herself.

What Isabella is afraid of, synonymous with her loss of virginity, is her loss of respect, both her own self-respect and the respect of the community. Her desire for "a more strict restraint / Upon the sisterhood" (1.4.4–5) must be linked with a strong fear of the consequences of integrating herself into a society dominated by exploitative men. In Irene Dash's terms, "In *Measure for Measure* Shakespeare again raises the question of woman's personal autonomy—her right to control her body." For Isabella, in light of the Vienna facing her, sexuality and self-esteem are mutually exclusive options. She has made her choice before she ever sets foot on stage. A woman in her position would not make such a decision without difficulty, even resentment. Isabella realizes that her "prosperous art," her ability to "play with reason and discourse" (1.2.184–85), would be wasted in the city. So she attempts to withdraw to the protective cloister—an option much missed by women in post-Reformation England. Just as Kate has taken "perverse refuge" behind the role of Shrew, Isabella tries to take refuge behind the role of Nun.

But just as Isabella is on the brink of forswearing the company of men, Lucio arrives to pull her back into it. Reluctantly she returns to Vienna, where, gradually, her character dissolves, her spirit erodes, and she becomes an obedient follower of male guidance: an actress in a male-dominated drama.

IV

If we examine Isabella's development in this play, we can see how her sense of self is undermined and finally destroyed through her encounters with patriarchal authority, an authority represented emphatically, but not exclusively, by the insensitive Duke. Her dilemma initially becomes apparent when she appears, a mere nun, before the Duke's appointed deputy. At first she is hesitant to assert herself against Angelo and is ready, at the slightest resistance, to give up her task of persuading him to free Claudio. But with Lucio's prompting, her "prosperous art" with words becomes evident. More and more masterfully she develops her argument, pleading eloquently for her brother's life:

> Go to your bosom,
> Knock there, and ask your heart what it doth know
> That's like my brother's fault. If it confess
> A natural guiltiness such as is his,
> Let it not sound a thought upon your tongue
> Against my brother's life.
>
> (2.2.136–41)

Even though at this early point in the play Isabella is already acting according to male direction, namely Lucio's, her integrity, which she so adamantly desires to protect, is still intact. Her voice remains, impressively, her own.

But Angelo assaults that integrity when he forces Isabella to choose between her brother's life and her maidenhood. He commands her, "Be that you are, / That is a woman," defining a woman's "destin'd livery" in no uncertain terms (2.4.134). As hard as she has tried to avoid understanding Angelo earlier in this scene, Isabella can now no longer claim to be ignorant of his "pernicious purpose" (1.150). When the deputy finally departs, leaving Isabella in the wake of his promise to torture her brother if she doesn't yield up her body to his will ("thy unkindness shall his death draw out / To ling'ring sufferance" [2.4.166–67]), she cries out in exasperation, "To whom shall I complain?" Her only hope for compassion lies with Claudio: "I'll to my brother," she declares, assured that there is at least one man in the world possessed of "a mind of honor" (2.171–79).

Naturally, when Claudio echoes Angelo's demands, arguing that Isabella's surrendering her virginity in this case would be a virtue, her frustration is exacerbated. She reacts the way a woman might if she had been raped and had found those closest to her unsympathetic; she feels isolated, hurt, terrified, enraged. Loss of virginity, after all, is never a light matter for Shakespeare's calumniated, or potentially calumniated, women. In *Much Ado about Nothing,* the perception of Hero as sexually tainted corresponds directly with the illusion of her as dead. For Isabella, too, the prospect of giving herself to Angelo is tantamount to dying: "Better it were a brother died at once, / Than that a sister . . . / Should die for ever" (2.4.106–8). If we understand how high the stakes are, we can hardly justify labeling Isabella a "vixen" when her strong will, until now subdued, gets the better of her and she swears,

> O you beast!
> O faithless coward! O dishonest wretch!
> . . . .
> Take my defiance!
> Die, perish! Might but my bending down
> Reprieve thee from thy fate, it should proceed.
> I'll pray a thousand prayers for thy death,
> No word to save thee.
>
> (3.1.135–46)

Her oaths here are far from endearing. But what they expose is neither rigidity nor coldness but a deeply rooted fear of exploitation, a fear justified by the attitudes toward women prevalent in this Vienna.

Claudio's urging Isabella to give up her virginity, understandable as it is from his point of view, compounds her increasing sense of vulnerability and helplessness.

Our experience of Isabella's being "thwarted here, there, and everywhere" is reinforced by the intervention of the Duke at precisely this troublesome point in the play. Although his intentions appear honorable at first, in his own way he replicates Angelo's and Claudio's indifference to Isabella's desire to remain true to herself. Like Angelo and Claudio before him, Vincentio sees in Isabella a reflection of his own needs. Consider his surprising endorsement of her attack on her brother. Rather than recoil at the harshness of her attack (as most of the play's critics have done), the Duke responds with delight: "The hand that hath made you fair hath made you good; the goodness that is cheap in beauty makes beauty brief in goodness; but grace, being the soul of your complexion, shall keep the body of it ever fair" (3.1.180–84). The Duke's perceptions of Isabella here reveal more about his character than about hers. What the Duke sees at this moment is the ideal woman that Hamlet never found: a woman who combines beauty and honesty; a woman who doesn't need to be told to get herself to a nunnery; a woman who represents the opposite of frailty. Unfortunately for Isabella, the Duke is so taken by his Hamletian fantasies that he fails to see the woman she really is—a woman in distress, who fears the very thing he will eventually require: the sacrifice of her autonomy.

Isabella's willingness to cooperate with the Duke's unscrupulous plot—and so to forfeit her autonomy—is clearly related to his choice of disguises. Vincentio, wearing Friar Francis's robe, has become the very thing he accuses Angelo of being: an "angel on the outward side" (3.2.272). Lucio is right to call him the "Duke of dark corners" (4.3.157). But whatever "crotchets" the Duke has in him (3.2.127), his disguise represents an authority that Isabella, as a nun, can hardly repudiate. When he invites her to fasten her ear on his advisings, she agrees to follow his direction. But like the provost, who protests that the Duke's order will force him to break an oath (4.2.181), Isabella makes it clear that she does not want to play any part that would require her to violate her personal sense of truth: "I have spirit to do any thing that appears not foul in the truth of my spirit" (3.1.205–7). She does not want to have to sacrifice her own voice.

But by the time the fourth act closes, the Duke has imposed on Isabella a role which goes against her wishes. As she explains to Mariana in the last scene of that act, "To speak so indirectly I am loath.

I would say truth" (2.1–2). However, because a supposed religious superior has instructed her to "veil full purpose" (1.4), she denies her personal inclinations and obeys the Duke without questioning. Neither green world nor cloister is available to Isabella now: she can neither subvert nor avoid the distorted value system which Vienna represents. She has no alternative but to submit to the Duke's authority. The Church, which was originally to function as Isabella's protector, has become her dictator. Even though she was able to resist both Angelo's attempt to ravish her body and Claudio's attempt to change her mind, Isabella is unable, finally, to resist the Duke's demands on her spirit.

V

This negation of Isabella's essentially self-defined character becomes complete upon the Duke's taking control of the action in act 3. Critics have noted this change variously. Richard Fly, for example, says that Isabella, "formerly an independent and authentic personality with a voice of her own," is "suddenly reduced to little more than a willing adjunct to the Duke's purpose." Clara Claiborne Park refers to Isabella as losing center stage. Whatever autonomy Isabella possessed in the beginning of the play, whatever "truth of spirit" she abided by, disintegrates once she agrees to serve in the Duke's plan. As soon as this "friar" takes over, Isabella becomes an actress whose words are no longer her own. There are no more outbursts. In complying with the role Vincentio has created for her, Isabella becomes his creation in a way that the male characters never do. When he presents her with the irreverent idea of the bed-trick, Isabella simply answers, "Show me how, good father" (3.1.238) and "The image of it gives me content already" (1.259). She cooperates with the Duke throughout the last act, in spite of her preference for "saying truth." When Angelo says that he perceives these "poor informal women" as "instruments of some more mightier member / That sets them on" (5.1.235–38), he doesn't know how truly he speaks.

The Duke claims, of course, to be acting in Isabella's best interests, just as he has claimed to be acting in the best interests of Vienna. He professes to be withholding the news that Claudio is alive in order to make Isabella "heavenly comforts of despair, / When it is least expected" (4.3.110–11). But the relationship between his professed intentions and the scenario he asks Isabella to act out is tenuous. In reward for her cooperation, Isabella has to kneel and swear in public that she, a recognized member of a local convent, "did yield" to the learned deputy (5.1.101)—a humiliating position to be forced into, no matter how cleverly the Duke may be intending to redeem her reputation. In retrospect, the Duke's promise to comfort Isabella—what Frye calls a "brutal lie"—appears to be a veiled justification for perpetuating his control over her. The passage in which the Duke urges Isabella to "pace" her wisdom "In that good path that [he] would wish it go"—a passage densely packed with imperatives (4.3.118–48)—is followed, significantly, by the entrance of the ego-puncturing Lucio. This juxtaposition of scenes should warn us not to take the Duke's proclaimed altruism at face value—just as the Duke's proclaimed aversion to staging himself to the people's eyes (1.1.68) belies *its* face value. Vincentio's grand opus, act 5—complete with trumpets to announce his entrance—is so conspicuously dramaturgical that it divides into a five-part structure. Clearly we are not to rest easy with this man's proclamations, nor should we be comfortable with the role he is asking Isabella to play.

Isabella's last words reveal just how far this imposed role diminishes her character. To those who argue that rather than depriving Isabella of autonomy the Duke is actually releasing her from moral rigidity by arranging for her to plead for Angelo's life, I answer that Isabella's final speech, often accepted as representing character growth, in fact represents the opposite. Ostensibly, Isabella is once again displaying her "prosperous art," using rhetoric to reveal a new-found capacity for mercy. But the quality of mercy here is strained:

> Most bounteous sir:
> Look, if it please you, on this man condemn'd
> As if my brother liv'd. I partly think
> A due sincerity governed his deeds,
> Till he did look on me. Since it is so,
> Let him not die. My brother had but justice,
> In that he did the thing for which he died;
> For Angelo,
> His act did not o'ertake his bad intent,
> And must be buried but as an intent
> That perish'd by the way. Thoughts are no subjects,
> Intents but merely thoughts.
>
> (5.1.443–54)

This speech lacks the integrity of Isabella's earlier speeches in which she pleaded with Angelo to ask his heart what it knew that was like her brother's fault. Logic, used so convincingly in the earlier speeches, has become twisted. For example, Isabella argues that since Claudio did "the thing for which he died" but Angelo did not commit the sin he thought he had, Angelo should not be punished. This argument is illogical because it wrongfully implies that evil actions, when carried out under mistaken circumstances, are harmless. If the crime had been misdirected murder, by this logic Isabella would have claimed that the act was no crime since the intended victim was still alive. Not only the laws of logic, but the concept of justice is twisted here. Isabella claims—as she need not—that her brother's supposed execution was, in fact, just. Her mode of argument is unsettling, not only because she sounds indifferent to Claudio's death, but also because she resorts to specious legalism where one would expect her to appeal to her faith, as she did when pleading for Claudio's salvation in 2.2.75–77:

> How would you be
> If He, which is the top of judgment, should
> But judge you as you are?

In comparison with this earlier speech, Isabella's final appeal represents not an increased but a stunted capacity for mercy. Her "prosperous art," subjected to the Duke's perverted dramaturgical efforts, has itself become perverted. Vincentio's charge—"trust not my holy order / If I pervert your course" (4.3.147–48)—becomes retrospectively ominous.

With the conclusion of her final speech, Isabella is immediately confronted with a series of overwhelming events: a living Claudio appears, the Duke proposes marriage, and Angelo is pardoned. All of Isabella's main assumptions—that Angelo was condemned, that the Duke was a committed celibate, that her brother was dead, and that she herself would remain chaste for life—are challenged, if not negated, in the space of five lines. She remains speechless, a baffled actress who has run out of lines. The gradual loss of her personal voice during the course of the play has become, finally, a literal loss of voice. In this sense, *Measure for Measure* is Isabella's tragedy. Like Lavinia in *Titus Andronicus*, the eloquent Isabella is left with no tongue.

VI

If we see Isabella as a victim of bad playwriting, we can compare her bewilderment at the end of *Measure for Measure* with our own. She has trusted the Duke, as we've trusted our playwright, to pattern events as he has led her to expect events to be patterned—and the Duke, sharing Shakespeare's affinity for surprises in this play, pulls those expectations out from under her. But by using Ragozine's head, for example—*caput ex machina*—to call attention to the ridiculousness of the Duke's machinations, Shakespeare simultaneously calls attention to his own superior skills. With this play Shakespeare has moved from comedy's romantic pole to its opposite, ironic, pole. What he has created in *Measure for Measure* is not a poorly written play, but, to some extent, a model for poor playwriting. (Such a model, clearly of abiding interest to Shakespeare, is less subtly depicted in the rustics' production of "Pyramus and Thisby" in *A Midsummer Night's Dream*.) By creating in Duke Vincentio a model third-rate playwright—one whose mind-set Jean Howard calls "confining, inelastic, dangerously reductive," one who has no qualms about "[draining] the life out of previously vital characters such as Isabella"—Shakespeare calls into question the ethics of his own craft, including the ethics involved in handling characters of the opposite sex. However, the extent to which Shakespeare transcends the Duke's limitations is not clear, especially with regard to the treatment of female characters. It is in this area that the comparison between the playwright and his surrogate becomes most murky.

Vincentio's sexual double standard is hardly subtle. Ever oblivious to female experience, Vincentio tells Juliet that because she returns Claudio's affection—because the "most offenseful act" is "mutually committed"—her sin is therefore "of heavier kind" than Claudio's (2.3.26–28). Such chauvinism, while present in Shakespeare's previous comedies, has almost always eventually been subverted in favor of mutuality. It would be tempting to claim that because the expected subversion of chauvinistic values does not occur in *Measure for Measure*, therefore Shakespeare must be consciously critiquing the Duke's double standard, once again—as in the case of Ragozine's head—showing himself to be the superior craftsman. But this claim would be ill-founded, considering that Shakespeare's own treatment of female characters at this point in his career becomes less than generous. As Vincentio "drains" life out of Isabella and Mariana, so Shakespeare drains life out of Gertrude and Ophelia, giving them scarcely any character at all. Joel Fineman's well-documented discussion of Shakespeare's "not uncommon defensive gynophobia," which erupts in certain tragedies, would support such an argument. If Shakespeare can be credited with critiquing Vincentio's treatment of female "characters," which seems unlikely, then he must also be said to be critiquing his treatment of some of his own.

But regardless of the playwright's intention, *Measure for Measure,* more than any of his previous plays, exposes the dehumanizing effect on women of living in a world dominated by powerful men who would like to re-create womanhood according to their fantasies. Duke Vincentio's distorted interpretation of Isabella's outrage in the prison scene is only one example of this kind of dehumanizing mind-set. His tampering with Isabella's character in act 5—which she must endure, according to religious edict—is no less a violation than Angelo's attempt to possess her body. As Hans Sachs puts it, the Duke succeeds in committing "in a legitimate and honorable way, the crime which Angelo attempted in vain."

This play reveals, among other things, the price women pay in order for male supremacy to be maintained. That price for Isabella is, precisely, a mandatory denial of her personal standards. But Isabella's plight is only one element in a larger pattern. As a whole, *Measure for Measure* explores the incompatibility of patriarchal and comic structures. The world of patriarchy, antithetical to the world of comedy throughout Shakespeare's works, comes closest here to overthrowing the comic world. Far from the one-dimensional representative of morality that critics have perceived her to be, Isabella is a key part of a dramatic environment in which the forces of patriarchy and comedy clash. In this context, her dramaturgical powerlessness becomes a variable in an equation in which the pervasiveness of chauvinism and the possibility of comic resolution are indirectly proportional. In other words, the stronger the forces of patriarchy, the less likely—or at least less convincing—comic resolution becomes.

Generically, Isabella is Shakespeare's pivotal female figure. She simultaneously links the dramatically effective early comic women to the victimized tragic women, even while her sympathetic portrayal anticipates the revival of influential women in the later plays. If Isabella's voice is lost in *Measure for Measure*—to remain mute throughout Shakespeare's tragedies, in which male misfortune and misogyny explode into significantly linked central issues—that voice is rediscovered in the romances, Shakespeare's most mature creations, in which patriarchal and misogynistic values, if present at all, are, as in the early comedies, subverted, and in which the imaginative environment once again allows female characters, like Paulina in *The Winter's Tale,* for example, to exert a powerful, positive force in shaping dramatic action.

Chronology

1564	William Shakespeare born at Stratford-on-Avon to John Shakespeare, a butcher, and Mary Arden. He is baptized on April 26.
1582	Marries Anne Hathaway in November.
1583	Daughter Susanna born, baptized on May 26.
1585	Twins Hamnet and Judith born, baptized on February 2.
1588–90	Sometime during these years, Shakespeare goes to London, without family. First plays performed in London.
1590–92	*The Comedy of Errors*, the three parts of *Henry VI*.
1593–94	Publication of *Venus and Adonis* and *The Rape of Lucrece*, both dedicated to the Earl of Southampton. Shakespeare becomes a sharer in the Lord Chamberlain's company of actors. *The Taming of the Shrew, The Two Gentlemen of Verona, Richard III*.
1595–97	*Romeo and Juliet, Richard II, King John, A Midsummer Night's Dream, Love's Labor's Lost*.
1596	Son Hamnet dies. Grant of arms to father.
1597	*The Merchant of Venice, Henry IV, Part 1*. Purchases New Place in Stratford.
1598–1600	*Henry IV, Part 2, As You Like It, Much Ado about Nothing, Twelfth Night, The Merry Wives of Windsor, Henry V*, and *Julius Caesar*. Moves his company to the new Globe Theatre.
1601	*Hamlet*. Shakespeare's father dies, buried on September 8.
1603	Death of Queen Elizabeth; James VI of Scotland becomes James I of England; Shakespeare's company becomes the King's Men.
1603–4	*All's Well That Ends Well, Measure for Measure, Othello*.

145

1605–6	*King Lear, Macbeth.*
1607	Marriage of daughter Susanna on June 5.
1607–8	*Timon of Athens, Antony and Cleopatra, Pericles.*
1608	Shakespeare's mother dies, buried on September 9.
1609	*Cymbeline,* publication of sonnets. Shakespeare's company purchases Blackfriars Theatre.
1610–11	*The Winter's Tale, The Tempest.* Shakespeare retires to Stratford.
1616	Marriage of daughter Judith on February 10. William Shakespeare dies at Stratford on April 23.
1623	Publication of the Folio edition of Shakespeare's plays.

Contributors

HAROLD BLOOM, Sterling Professor of the Humanities at Yale University, is the author of *The Anxiety of Influence, Poetry and Repression,* and many other volumes of literary criticism. His forthcoming study, *Freud: Transference and Authority,* attempts a full-scale reading of all of Freud's major writings. A MacArthur Prize Fellow, he is general editor of five series of literary criticism published by Chelsea House. During 1987–88, he was appointed Charles Eliot Norton Professor of Poetry at Harvard University.

M. C. BRADBROOK is a Fellow of Girton College, Cambridge, and is the recipient of numerous awards and honorary degrees. She has written extensively on Shakespeare and Elizabethan literature.

HAROLD C. GODDARD was Head of the English Department at Swarthmore College from 1909 to 1946. He is remembered not only for *The Meaning of Shakespeare,* but also for his writings upon American Transcendentalism.

A. P. ROSSITER was Lecturer in English at Cambridge University and the author of *Angel with Horns.*

HERBERT WELL, Jr., is Professor of English and Head of the Department at the University of Manitoba. He has written numerous essays on Shakespeare, including "The Options of the Audience" and "Shakespeare in the Theatre."

HARRIET HAWKINS is Professor of English at Vassar College. She is the author of *Likenesses of Truth in Elizabethan and Restoration Drama* and *Poetic Freedom and Poetic Truth: Chaucer, Shakespeare, Marlowe, and Milton.*

LOUISE SCHLEINER is professor of English at the University of California at Davis. She is the author of *The Living Lyre in English Verse from Elizabeth through The Restoration*.

PHOEBE S. SPINRAD teaches at Louisiana State University.

MARCIA RIEFER teaches at Syracuse University. She has published various short stories and directed or assisted in directing several plays with the Contemporary Theatre of Syracuse.

Bibliography

Bache, William B. Measure for Measure *as Dialectical Art*. Lafayette: Purdue University Press, 1969.

Battenhouse, Roy W. "*Measure for Measure* and Christian Doctrine of the Atonement." *PMLA* 61 (1946): 1029–59.

Bennett, Josephine W. Measure for Measure *as Royal Entertainment*. New York: Columbia University Press, 1966.

Birje-Patil, J. "Marriage Contracts in Shakespeare's *Measure for Measure*." *Shakespeare Survey* 5 (1969): 106–11.

Black, James. "The Unfolding of *Measure for Measure*." *Shakespeare Survey* 26 (1973): 119–28.

Caputi, Anthony. "Scenic Design in *Measure for Measure*." *Journal of English and Germanic Philology* 40 (1961): 423–34.

Coghill, Nevill. "Comic Form in *Measure for Measure*." *Shakespeare Survey* 8 (1955): 14–27.

Cole, Howard C. "The 'Christian' Context of *Measure for Measure*." *Journal of English and Germanic Philology* 64 (1965): 425–51.

Cox, John D. "The Medieval Background of *Measure for Measure*." *Modern Philology* 81 (1983): 1–13.

Dunkel, Wilbur. "Law and Equity in *Measure for Measure*." *Shakespeare Quarterly* 13 (1962): 275–85.

Frye, Northrop. *A Natural Perspective: The Development of Shakespearean Comedy and Romance*. New York: Harcourt Brace, 1965.

Gelb, Hal. "Duke Vincentio and the Illusion of Comedy." *Shakespeare Quarterly* 22 (1971): 25–34.

Gless, Darryl J. Measure for Measure, *the Law and the Convent*. Princeton: Princeton University Press, 1979.

Hawkins, Hariett. *Likenesses of Truth in Elizabethan and Restoration Drama*. Oxford: Clarendon Press, 1972.

Hunter, G. K. "Six Notes on *Measure for Measure*." *Shakespeare Quarterly* 15 (1964): 167–72.

Hunter, Robert G. *Shakespeare and the Comedy of Forgiveness*. New York: Columbia University Press, 1965.

Kirsch, Arthur. "The Integrity of *Measure for Measure*." *Shakespeare Survey* 28 (1975): 89–105.

Knight, G. Wilson. *The Wheel of Fire*. London: Oxford University Press, 1930.

Knights, L. C. "The Ambiguity of *Measure for Measure*." *Scrutiny* 10 (1942): 222–33.

Lascelles, Mary. *Shakespeare's* Measure for Measure. London: Athlone, 1953.

Lawrence, William W. *Shakespeare's Problem Comedies*. London: Macmillan, 1937. Reprint. Harmondsworth and Baltimore: Penguin, 1969.

Leavis, F. R. *The Common Pursuit*. London: Chatto & Windus, 1952.

Leech, Clifford. "The 'Meaning' of *Measure for Measure*." *Shakespeare Survey* 3 (1950): 66–73.

Miles, Rosalind. *The Problem of* Measure for Measure. New York: Barnes & Noble, 1976.

Mincoff, Marco. "*Measure for Measure:* A Question of Approach." *Shakespeare Survey* 2 (1966): 141–52.

Muir, Kenneth. *Shakespeare Sources*. London: Methuen, 1957.

Nagarajan, S., ed. *Measure for Measure*. Signet Shakespeare. New York: Signet, 1964.

Owen, Lucy. "Mode and Character in *Measure for Measure*." *Shakespeare Quarterly* 25 (1974): 17–32.

Pope, Elizabeth M. "The Elizabethan Background of *Measure for Measure*." *Shakespeare Survey* 2 (1966): 66–82.

Schanzer, Ernest. "The Marriage-Contracts in *Measure for Measure*." *Shakespeare Survey* 13 (1960): 81–89.

———. *The Problem Plays of Shakespeare*. London: Routledge and Kegan Paul, 1963.

Skura, Meredith. "New Interpretations for Interpretation in *Measure for Measure*." *boundary 2* 7 (1979): 39–59.

Stevenson, David L. *The Achievement of Shakespeare's* Measure for Measure. Ithaca: Cornell University Press, 1966.

———. "*Design and Structure in* Measure for Measure." *ELH* 23 (1956): 256–78.

Tillyard, E. M. W. *Shakespeare's Problem Plays*. Toronto: University of Toronto Press, 1949.

Van Laan, Thomas F. *Role-Playing in Shakespeare*. Toronto: University of Toronto Press, 1978.

Westlund, Joseph. *Shakespeare's Reparative Comedies: A Psychoanalytic View of the Middle Plays*. Chicago: University of Chicago Press, 1984.

Wheeler, Richard. *Shakespeare's Development and the Problem Comedies: Turn and Counter-Turn*. Berkeley: University of California Press, 1981.

Acknowledgments

"Authority, Truth, and Justice in *Measure for Measure*" by M. C. Bradbrook from *The Review of English Studies* 17, no. 68 (October 1941), © 1941 by Oxford University Press. Reprinted by permission.

"Power in *Measure for Measure*" (originally entitled "*Measure for Measure*") by Harold C. Goddard from *The Meaning of Shakespeare* by Harold C. Goddard, © 1951 by the University of Chicago. Reprinted by permission of the University of Chicago Press.

"*Measure for Measure*" by A. P. Rossiter from *Angel with Horns: Fifteen Lectures on Shakespeare*, edited by Graham Storey, © 1961 by Longman, Green & Co. Ltd. Reprinted by permission.

"Form and Contexts in *Measure for Measure*" by Herbert Weil, Jr., from *The Critical Quarterly* 12, no. 1 (Spring 1970), © 1970 by Herbert Weil, Jr. Reprinted by permission.

"The Devil's Party: Virtues and Vices in *Measure for Measure*" by Harriett Hawkins from *Shakespeare Survey* 31 (1978), © 1978 by Cambridge University Press. Reprinted by permission of Cambridge University Press.

"Providential Improvisation in *Measure for Measure*" by Louise Schleiner from *PMLA* 97, no. 2 (March 1982), © 1982 by the Modern Language Association of America. Reprinted by permission of the Modern Language Association of America.

"*Measure for Measure* and the Art of Not Dying" by Phoebe Spinrad from *Texas Studies in Literature and Language* 26, no. 1 (Spring 1984), © 1984 by University of Texas Press. Reprinted by permission of the author and the University of Texas Press.

" 'Instruments of Some More Mightier Member': The Constriction of Female Power in *Measure for Measure*" by Marcia Riefer from *Shakespeare Quarterly* 35, no. 2 (Summer 1984), © 1984 by the Folger Shakespeare Library. Reprinted by permission of *Shakespeare Quarterly*, and its publisher, The Folger Shakespeare Library.

151

Index